NEW YORK REVIEW BOOKS
CLASSICS

POLITICAL ACTION

MICHAEL WALZER is a professor emeritus at the Institute
for Advanced Study in Princeton. He served as the co-editor of
the political journal *Dissent* for more than three decades and
has written about a wide variety of topics in political theory and
moral philosophy. His most recent book is *A Foreign Policy for
the Left*.

JON WIENER is the host and producer of *Start Making Sense*,
The Nation's weekly podcast, and a longtime contributing
editor at *The Nation*. He is a professor emeritus of history at
the University of California, Irvine, and his most recent book
is *How We Forgot the Cold War: A Historical Journey Across
America*.

POLITICAL ACTION

A Practical Guide to Movement Politics

MICHAEL WALZER

Introduction by
JON WIENER

NEW YORK REVIEW BOOKS

New York

THIS IS A NEW YORK REVIEW BOOK
PUBLISHED BY THE NEW YORK REVIEW OF BOOKS
435 Hudson Street, New York, NY 10014
www.nyrb.com

Copyright © 1971 by Michael Walzer; new preface copyright © 2019 by
Michael Walzer
Introduction copyright © 2019 by Jon Wiener
All rights reserved.

Library of Congress Cataloging-in-Publication Data
Names: Walzer, Michael, author.
Title: Political action : a practical guide to movement politics / by Michael
    Walzer ; introduction by Jon Wiener ; preface by Michael Walzer.
Description: New York : New York Review Books, [2019] | Series: New York
    Review Books Classics
Identifiers: LCCN 2018052228| ISBN 9781681373539 (alk. paper) | ISBN
    9781681373546 (epub)
Subjects: LCSH: Politics, Practical. | Political participation.
Classification: LCC JF2049 .W25 2019 | DDC 322.4—dc23
LC record available at https://lccn.loc.gov/2018052228

ISBN 978-1-68137-353-9
Available as an electronic book; ISBN 978-1-68137-354-6

Printed in the United States of America on acid-free paper.
10 9 8 7 6 5 4 3 2 1

CONTENTS

INTRODUCTION

THE IDEA of republishing this book came from some high-school students in Los Angeles. They were part of a social justice group at their school, and most of the projects they were contemplating involved organizing of some kind. To help them think about that, their faculty adviser, Mickey Morgan, a former student of Michael Walzer (and a friend of mine), photocopied parts of *Political Action* and handed it out. "This is really good!" they told him. "This is what we need." It spoke to them, Mickey said, "with its seriousness and straightforwardness and by not being fancy or 'theoretical,'" and because the author's voice was "so human and thoughtful."

What the kids said next became the impetus for this new edition: "Why is there nothing like this?" Mickey told me about it and said, "I can keep handing out photocopies, but really somebody should reprint the book."

I found my paperback original from 1971. (Although the title had disappeared from the spine, the author's name was still there.) It wasn't hard to see what they liked about the book. But, I asked, weren't the kids bothered by the absence of any mention of social media? "No," Mickey said. "They know all about doing politics on social media—they don't have to be told." They know it's easy to like and share Facebook posts and to retweet good tweets. But of course they are sharing with and tweeting to people who are already their friends or followers. The kids understood the real problem: In order to get people to join your Facebook group and subscribe to your organization's Twitter feed and follow your project's Instagram page, you need to find them and convince them to join. Social media is a key tool for staying in touch with people once you've signed them up. But first, you have to talk to them. You have to persuade the apathetic and educate the ignorant and give hope and maybe even inspiration to those who are discouraged and depressed about politics. The talking part is the key, and it's the hardest—and it's why the kids found this book so valuable.

Although the question of the hour, and the year, is what is to be done about Trump, how to defeat him and his supporters in the next election, the students also liked the book because it was "not just about how to do electoral politics. It's about anything you do that involves working in the community." Of course they're right. Today, for many of Mickey's students, climate change is the biggest concern, and the one they are most passionate to try to do something about.

Then Mickey invited me to talk to the group. I told them that the emphasis in electoral politics today is not on face-to-face canvassing and local organizing. Campaigns are focused above all on fund-raising, most of which goes for television ads. Of course these days it takes huge amounts of money to run for office—contested Senate races in 2016 cost on the average almost $20 million, with about half coming from super PACs. The average House race in 2016 cost $1.5 million. That's why candidates spend almost all their time fund-raising, most of it on the phone, calling big donors. After paying for television ads, the rest of the money is largely spent on polling and on consultants—the ones who say fund-raising is everything.

But political scientists have come to a different conclusion from the consultants. Most of the research has concluded that face-to-face, person-to-person conversations are by far the most effective way to persuade the doubters, inform the ignorant, and win new supporters. One-on-one talking is far more effective than television ads. Is anyone surprised by this? It's hard work for candidates to raise money from big donors, but it's even harder to run a strong ground game, to organize teams of volunteers going door to door, week after week, keeping track of who they've talked to, and getting back to supporters when the polls open.

Since 1971, when Michael Walzer wrote this book, many things have changed in American politics. But the situation we face today bears some striking similarities to the Vietnam years, above all, the question of what we can do, what we should do, about a president who fills us with dread and rage. "What is to be done?" is of course the classic question for leftists facing oppressive regimes and long odds. Those high-school kids thought there was a good answer in Walzer's book; it is, as Walzer writes, "an invitation to commitment and participation," to get together in groups, to argue at meetings, and then to go out and talk to people.

So I sent my old copy to Edwin Frank at New York Review Books Classics, suggesting they reprint it. He replied, "That seems like a good idea."

—JON WIENER

PREFACE TO THE 2019 EDITION

WRITTEN almost fifty years ago, in the immediate aftermath of the American bombing of Cambodia, this book reflects a decade of intense political activity. Since I was aiming at a guide that would be helpful to citizen activists of all sorts, I avoided specific references to sixties politics; I wrote in a generalizing mode. But now I want to describe to new readers some of the concrete engagements that made me a citizen activist and led me to write *Political Action*.

Movement politics is mostly the work of the young, and I was very young, twenty-five, an unhappy graduate student, when Irving Howe, the editor of *Dissent*, asked me to fly to North Carolina and talk to and write about the black college students who were sitting in at Woolworth lunch counters. It was February 1960, and the sit-ins were the beginning of The Sixties.

I did talk to the students and write about them, but what was more important, I helped organize, with other liberals and leftists in the Boston area, the Emergency Public Integration Committee (EPIC), whose members picketed local Woolworth stores in solidarity with the Southern sit-inners. EPIC started with a good name, which is important, and at its peak was running demonstrations in front of some forty stores in and around Boston. A friend and fellow graduate student was the organizing genius behind all this; I mostly talked, explained what we were doing, recruited picketers at the region's many universities—and struggled to ward off ideologues on the farther left, who wanted EPIC to make a revolution. I also consulted with lawyers and, together with the picket-line captains, negotiated with the police, who were mostly unfriendly but careful and correct, and who didn't harass the picketers so long as we didn't harass the shoppers.

Ours was a single-issue politics. We knew that racism in the United States reached far beyond whites-only lunch counters, segregated restrooms, and back-of-the-bus seating, but we followed the students in the South; we were not an independent movement. EPIC had a short life; after 1960, Northern supporters of the civil rights movement went South, marched in Alabama rather than in Boston. And of course we marched in Washington, too, and listened, standing there or on the radio, to Martin Luther King Jr.'s famous "I Have a Dream" speech. But it might have been more effective in the long run had we sustained local organizations in the North where racism was less visible, perhaps, but a powerful force nonetheless. So I began to think about how activists, such as we were, could keep things going.

A large number of civil rights activists moved naturally into the anti–Vietnam War movement. That was my next political destination and, again, my most intense engagement was local. By the mid-sixties, we had a new model for local political action: Students for a Democratic Society (SDS) community organizing. In 1967, I joined with a few people from Harvard SDS to organize the Cambridge Neighborhood Committee on Vietnam (CNCV), whose aim was to mobilize the city of Cambridge against the war. We went house to house, block by block, talking to whoever would talk to us, looking for someone who would volunteer to host a neighborhood meeting where we could defend the antiwar position.

Community organizing, SDS-style, required us to find "community people" and make them the leaders of the organization. This could be an inauthentic politics, where the young activists sat in the back of the room while a community person ran the meeting, and the people attending got cricks in their necks looking back for cues from the real leaders. But that wasn't the case in CNCV. One of our early volunteers was a part-time film editor and young mother who turned out to understand more about organizing than any of the rest of us—and who went from the CNCV to law school and a distinguished career in civil liberties work. I was her co-chair, who talked, probably too much, at our frequent meetings and fended off the Trotskyists.

Every organization needs a project; activists can't just talk; they have to find something to do. So we circulated petitions to put a statement on the November ballot calling on the city of Cambridge to hold a one-day rally against the war. With the help of a friendly lawyer, we got on the ballot, and then went door to door asking for votes. Looking for help, we gathered our courage and invited King to come to Cambridge and knock on a door. He came and knocked in front of reporters and cameras, and briefly we brought the civil rights and antiwar movements together (but only a few of the black preachers followed King's lead).

I doubt that King helped us in the white ethnic neighborhoods of Cambridge. We got 40 percent of the vote in November, and lost every working-class district. Only Harvard Square and its immediate surround voted strongly against the war. We recruited a few community people but hardly made a dent in the larger community. Still, CNCV had established a presence in at least part of Cambridge and might have survived as a political organization, reaching out to other issues and seeking a wider base (a few people suggested that we run a candidate for city council). But that was not to be.

Political activity requires a lot of work, and the distribution of the work is a central issue, not because activists try to avoid the burden but because they are too eager to embrace it. The younger activists, even if they are students or instructors (as I was) in supposedly demanding universities, have a lot of time for all sorts of organizational work and especially for meetings. The community people are older, with jobs and families; their time for political action is limited. So the young sit through long meetings, work long hours, and take over. But we were, most of us, without community roots and with very strong ideological commitments. As the war in Vietnam escalated, became morally unbearable, we started arguing among ourselves about what ought to be done. We had no particular interest in Cambridge city politics; indeed, the war made local politics look less and less important. We were drawn into national debates, and in these debates we took different sides. So CNCV died of division.

Some of us went into draft resistance; a very few joined the Weathermen and tried "to bring the war home"; most of us supported the presidential campaign of Eugene McCarthy (as I did). I traveled briefly with McCarthy and made notes for some of his speeches (and he wrote a foreword for the original edition of this book). Not all citizen movements have to end with electoral politics, but I thought that was the right end for the antiwar movements of the late sixties. Our central obligation was simply to stop the war, as McCarthy would have done—and probably Robert Kennedy, too, who stepped in late in the day and added to the divisions on the left. His assassination led to Hubert Humphrey's nomination and then the disastrous defeat of 1968.

What followed was the invasion of Cambodia, ordered by Richard Nixon and Henry Kissinger—which produced another big Washington march but no renewal of local antiwar politics. The divisions on the political and intellectual left were deep and, so it seemed, irreconcilable. For the moment, I had nothing to do, and when political activists can't act, they write a book.

The editors at New York Review Books Classics have agreed to republish this book exactly as I wrote it in 1970–71, with all my incorrectly gendered pronouns. But I think that I was more aware than most sixties activists of the central role that women should play in our organizations. This isn't a period piece. Perhaps the only chapter that would need revision today is the one on the mass media, which deals with relations between activists and reporters. None of us anticipated the anarchy of the Internet, where thousands of people are posting and tweeting every day. What looks like participatory democracy has led, instead, to radical polarization and endless falsification. No doubt, the new media can help raise money and, maybe, get people to a demonstration; they can be used to spread the word about a new organizing effort—as in the aftermath of the shooting at Marjory Stoneman Douglas High School. But I don't believe that they can replace the face-to-face encounters that build and sustain movement politics. It is still necessary to get together in small groups, to argue at meetings, to knock on doors, to talk and to listen to your neighbors—which is what *Political Action* is about.

Every author dreams of a second life for his or her books, and I am grateful to be granted this one. Every political activist who has fought for a good cause dreams of a chance to fight again. We live, right now, in a bad time; American politics has not been this ugly since the Joe McCarthy years or the Red Scare and anti-immigrant frenzy of the early 1920s. We need movements of resistance, and we need citizen activists who remember the old labor union imperative: Organize!

—MICHAEL WALZER
August 2018

PREFACE TO THE 1971 EDITION

I WROTE most of this little book in the weeks immediately following the American invasion of Cambodia, almost a year ago. It is a political response to that event and to the outburst of citizen activism that followed. I want to emphasize that it is far more the work of an amateur activist than of a professional political scientist. I cannot claim much detachment from the people whose politics is described and (often) criticized in these pages. The criticisms are ones I have actually made or listened to other people make at meetings, and I have not hesitated to reproduce the hope, the anger, the weariness that my friends and I—and doubtless our opponents too—felt at such moments. It is my purpose to recommend political action of a certain sort, not political action in general, to my readers. The best way to do that, it seems to me, is simply to join the debates that go on every day in citizens' clubs and movements.

I have encountered one difficulty that ought to be mentioned here. There is no classical history of citizen politics to which I can refer. Even movements of national scope are too little known in their details to serve as easy references. In any case, my own experience is with local activism, of little interest except to fellow participants in this or that project. So I have often failed to be concrete, though many readers will surely be able to supplement my advice with experiences that will serve (I hope) to confirm it.

Citizen politics is not an affair of lonely leaders or abstracted theorists. It is a roughly equalitarian and highly sociable activity, and one gets along, if at all, with a lot of help from one's friends. I have had help writing this book, most especially from Carolyn Grace, Irving Howe, Martin Peretz, and Judith Walzer, comrades in different enterprises.

—MICHAEL WALZER
January 1971

POLITICAL ACTION

for Sarah and Rebecca
whether they choose to be activists
or not

1. THE POLITICAL MOMENT

A GREAT deal of political activity is routine day-in, day-out work, best left to professionals. Other people don't have time for it, though they are often doing work very much like it in organizations whose character is not overtly political. But routine performances are adequate only to routine occasions. In moments of crisis, the professionals often can't cope; or, given new perceptions of injury and injustice, they seem to be coping badly. Then the democratic system offers a standing invitation to the rest of us to enlist in political life, an invitation to commitment and participation. More rarely, the question is not of enlistment but conscription: the routines suddenly collapse, and harsh choices are forced upon large numbers of men and women.

One of the reasons the choices are so harsh is that they involve people in activity and movement who were passive before. These are not incompetent people (not all or most of them, anyway), but they are often innocent of the complications of political life. They are unaware of the personal risks involved, unprepared for enmity and contention, unaccustomed to the sheer endlessness of artful talk and manipulative behavior. Nevertheless, they act. In clubs, campaigns, movements, they articulate their sense of *something wrong* and press for change. This little handbook is for them, because they are inexpert, as I am, and in order that the little we learn will not become a trade secret.

Every man has his own sense of crisis and outrage. So long as this is not shared or widely shared, most of us deal with it, suffer from it, repress and forget it, in private. The solitary prophet makes his own wilderness of inattention, mockery, and withdrawal by talking to people unwilling to listen. It is (sometimes) worth trying, but most of us learn to keep quiet. Political action is only possible when expressions of outrage and prophecies of disaster meet a lively response, at least within some circle of our own acquaintances. We try them out on our friends. The actual decision to enter the political arena will almost certainly be made by a small group, but it should only be made by a group whose members have what might be called intimations of growth. Where do such intimations come from? Hopefully, from conversations and encounters with other people, hints of commitment, plausible signs of interest. Would-be activists must have some sense of their future constituency; they must know that so many people will support the strike, attend the mass meeting, join the march, before they put themselves forward and call for action.

I want to caution against the intimations of pure theory, the products of a very specialized form of conversation. Political discourse carried on within the narrow circle of academies and sects does not produce—not alone—signs sufficient to justify political action. Later on, I will take up some of the problems of sectarian politics, but one feature of such politics should be mentioned here: the willingness to act, in disregard of present experience, on the basis of one or another theoretical view of the future. Then parties and movements are developed that are grounded on nothing more than the tense expectancy of the faithful, and barring the occurrence of the expected events, and given the likely occurrence of unexpected events, the band of the faithful generally remains small. There are ways of dealing with this difficulty, as the long history of Christianity suggests, but there are many more ways of not dealing with it. Hence the political sects of the Left, each one the product of an initiative for which, whatever the verdict of the future, the present was not ripe.

But sectarian initiatives are at least preceded by extended speculations about consequences and outcomes. Much more dangerous is the recklessness suggested by the maxim of a Jacobin leader in 1793: *"On s'engage et puis, on voit."* I commit myself, and then ... I see what happens. That is, whether or not I have support, whether or not my commitment is retrievable, whether or not other people are affected, and, if so, how they are affected, I act in the hope of unpredictable goods and even, perhaps, without any hope at all. What this most often means is that my action derives from personal rage and frustration so intense, so unbearable that doing something now seems far more urgent than producing effects later on. I have, in fact, had such feelings, and I have seen other people possessed by them. But political motivation is something quite different. We become political men when we act for public and not private reasons, or at least for public in addition to private reasons, and when we imagine our effects in terms of other people as well as ourselves. Political action is action with or for others, and while we may think our personal feelings very important (as we all do), they are, in fact, less important than the inevitably impersonal feelings for other people that are involved in acting with this group, for this group, against that group of men and women whom we cannot really know.

Large numbers of men and women ready to act together without knowing one another, and in disregard of the professional and his routines—these are the makings of the political moment. The makers of the moment are some smaller number of men and women who recognize the readiness and give it public expression. The readiness itself has two sources. Common injury, class interest, ethnic solidarity produce a kind of citizen politics most likely to evolve into professionalism, most likely to leave behind permanent defensive alliances and associations. Only the beginning moments of the labor movement (and then of each new union), for instance, provide clear examples of amateur activism—though every strike turns up new activists free of professional sophistication yet politically competent in surprising ways. On the other hand, the struggle for women's suffrage remained throughout a citizens' movement and never produced a professionally run feminist union, in part because no ongoing organization of women was (or was thought to be) necessary once suffrage was won.

Moral outrage, anger, and sorrow for injustices done within our own society, or by our government overseas, produce a kind of citizen politics most likely to remain the province of citizens, largely because its incidence and endurance are so unpredictable. Professional politicians seek out, sometimes, the support of such citizens, but they are not likely to join them. In any case, the politicians are rarely there at the beginning. The first attempts to cope with the crisis, to end the injustice, begin without them, and despite them, when a group of citizens holds a meeting, argues about strategies, and plans a new organization.

2. BEGINNINGS

THE FIRST task is to find the support one believes is there, to reach out somehow to unknown but sympathetic people. In order to do that, the little group of activists must appear to be more than it yet is. Beginnings are rarely straightforward; they trade on unpredictable futures. It is necessary at once that there be a name, a speculation on the movement to follow, but worth thinking about, since names are not easy to change. After the name, an address, a letterhead, a list of sponsors, a statement and a program, a press release. All this may seem embarrassing and pretentious to the men and women who put it together; they can still meet, and probably will, in each other's living rooms. But there is no other way. They must make themselves visible, and it is not enough simply to stand up.

Political movements are begun by throwing together a façade, behind which activists rush about trying to raise a building. Often enough, they fail; the façade collapses before there is any shelter behind it. But if they have chosen their moment wisely, the first little group will find people to help it along. Other groups will spring up on the same model and will want to affiliate with the first, not necessarily because it is larger or more powerful, but simply because it is first. The initiative belongs to its members, as do, for a time at least, the crucial decisions.

Sometimes the original group is already a political association—a sect or party—and its members are political professionals, though most likely of a marginal sort. Then the
façade they put up is especially important. They must look
like ordinary citizens if they are to attract significant support. This sort of disguise should probably be encouraged;
in many cases it is the functional equivalent of good intentions. And, assuming a worthwhile cause and an attractive
façade, even knowledgeable activists may do well to join, for
the sake of the others, so to speak; and, if necessary, to make
trouble later on.

With regard to many issues, national committees of one
sort or another already exist, founded, sometimes, long ago,
and sustained with more loyalty than wisdom. Nevertheless,
it is often sensible to try to begin under the banner of an
established organization and to work with or (in time) take
over its national office. Otherwise, energy will be wasted
differentiating oneself from the existing group and fighting
with its staff. There is often real help to be had, and the
status of a local branch is nothing to be ashamed of. But if
the existing group has come to be identified with defeat, or
with some idiosyncratic and isolated leader, or with sectarian styles of political action, then not only a fresh start but
also the appearance of a fresh start is vitally necessary. Citizen activists gain a great deal, in such cases, if their movement
looks shiny and new.

3. STRATEGIC CHOICES

QUIET men and women often exaggerate the importance of their own outrage, their long delayed decision to *do something*. If they are moved, how can the rest of the world stand still? But it is always best to plan one's moves on the supposition that most of the world will stand still, that established institutions and social practices will survive the shock. All that has changed is that some group of people has decided to use the pronoun "we," and to act together. Nor is it the case in a democratic society that this decision challenges the political system. Quiet citizens are the resources of a democracy, saved up, we are told, for those moments when professionalism fails. They may feel unconventional; they may behave unconventionally; but their intermittent forays into the political arena are by now one of the conventions of democratic politics. That doesn't mean that what they do isn't important, nor that it isn't sometimes dangerous. Using democratic rights puts them at risk: now there are men and women—now there are enemies—threatened by that use. For this reason above all, it is important for activists to know what they can and cannot do, and never to indulge themselves (or frighten their enemies) with fantasies of social and political changes they cannot actually bring about.

Revolution is such a fantasy, less common than is often thought, but worth dealing with early on. Citizen activists may aim at this or that fundamental change, but they cannot hope to make a revolution. It is not very often that anyone actually *makes* a revolution. Revolutions happen, and all sorts of people find themselves, unexpectedly, participants in the happening. Ordinary citizens will be among them (often yearning not to be), but at such moments it is the professionals, newly recruited professionals perhaps, who take charge. Power of the ultimate sort is at stake, and no one contends for such power in a part-time way, or carries on simultaneously a nonpolitical career, or retires casually from the struggle once some point of special interest has been won. But these are the characteristics of citizen activists; simply listing them helps explain why amateur politics is most often parasitic on the routines of a more or less stable democratic system. The crises and outrages that set off the political activity of ordinary citizens are serious enough, but they occur within a system that is not yet in a state of total crisis and that protects even the irregular responses of its members. Most men and women join the movement counting on that protection. It isn't absolute, as they will learn, but it is a great deal more than revolutionaries have any right to expect.

Giving the system a "last chance" is another fantasy. This suggests that revolution is the next step if citizen activism in general, or this particular citizens' campaign, fails to carry the cause to victory. But activists have no business imagining that they will win right away; they are a minority, probably a small minority, of the country. They must risk failure, and they ought to be aware that the most likely consequence of failure is not revolution at all, but the fragmentation of their movement and the retreat of many citizens from politics. Small bands of sectarian militants may then experiment with disruption and violence, fantastically imitating Jacobins and Bolsheviks. But this is rarely a serious business. One day, hopefully, there will be a new mobilization of activists, a reorganized movement, and another citizens' campaign—that is, another "last chance" for the system. *There is nothing else to do but try again.*

The real choice faced by the men and women who plan these successive attempts is between two kinds of politics, both of which have conventional names, though they can each be pursued in a variety of irregular ways. The two kinds are pressure politics and electoral politics, and I am inclined to think that there are no other kinds. To choose pressure politics means to try to influence those people who already hold power, who sit in official seats, who may even be responsible for the outrages against which the movement is aimed. To choose electoral politics is to try to dislodge those people and plant others in their seats, not necessarily or even probably the leaders of the movement, more likely whatever alternative set of professional politicians the system provides. Of course, the two choices overlap in important ways; they are often pursued simultaneously, with stress being put on the first only until some group of professionals adopts the cause. But it is worth emphasizing the two simply because they exhaust the range: changing the policies men make and changing the men who make policies. Changing the political system within which policy is made is rarely a real option for citizen activists.

It is never easy to know when to shift from pressure to electoral politics, whether at any given moment (and the moments are recurrent) to enter or to avoid the campaign of this or that candidate or party. On the one hand, electioneering is the sort of politics citizen activists are most familiar with, know best, probably do best. On the other hand, they often feel that their break with the routines of the system precludes it. They have come to distrust the promises of professional politicians. They are in search precisely of a politics that does not require them to support candidates who are only barely better than their opponents and who have, most likely, weak and vacillating positions on what the activists believe is the crucial issue. Sentiment of this sort is entirely justified. It is, after all, what makes the movement possible in the first place.

But assuming that pressure politics (petitions, mass meetings, marches, and so on) doesn't lead to a change in government policy, electoral politics is a necessary next step. The movement can't avoid it, even if supporting conventional candidates and parties involves some compromise of its principles. It is only a question of when, and to that there is no specific answer. The general answer is: not until the movement is strong enough to force fairly clear positions upon the professionals and to exercise some control over them once they have won.

This general rule sometimes suggests to activists that they must run their own candidates or that they must join in a new political party. A single-issue educational campaign, even with victory inconceivable, may be a useful activity; whether it is or isn't in any particular case is a tactical decision. A new party is something quite different. It involves the movement in a coalition with many other groups and so defines its position on many other issues; it requires a commitment to an elaborate program and to broad social change. That is a commitment many of the activists would probably like to make, but it is not what first brought them together, and it is not what holds them together with other activists in the movement. Nor is it at all clear that a new party and a struggle for social change on a wide front is the best (the easiest or the quickest) way to carry their own cause to victory. There are, in fact, two very different strategies entangled here, which will have to be separated out in the course of movement debate and action. Two questions are crucial: Should the citizens' movement be committed to single-issue or to multi-issue politics? Should the movement be organized as a single constituency or a coalition?

4. DEFINING THE ISSUES

NEW POLITICAL movements generally take shape around
a single issue—a wrong being done to the people who join
or to some other group with whom they have political connections or moral sympathies. The activists are likely to
disagree about much else, but this sense of injury or indignation they must share. As they work together, they may come
to share more than this. Issues related to the original one
come into view, and the values that underlay their first choice
of action may lead them to choose again, to extend the range
of their movement. Sometimes, however, and probably more
often, new issues have opposite effects: the movement splin-
ters; its members discover that they are really radically different from one another.

These different possibilities lead from the first to very
different views of what the movement should be like. Some
members insist that its focus should be resolutely fixed on
the single issue that brought them together. Necessarily they
attribute great importance to that issue: they believe or they
say that the world will be different (and much better) once
it is resolved. They blind themselves, sometimes willfully, to
the entanglements of social and political life, to all the ob-
stacles that lie between the particular victory they may in
fact win and the transformations they hope for. They choose
the part over the whole; that is, they have or choose to have

perceptions of the part, but only visions of the whole. Other members seem to be more realistic. They try to fit the single issue into a complex of problems. They try to develop a coherent program for social or political change. Then they want the movement to adopt their program, to switch from single-issue to multi-issue politics. Perhaps that means that some activists will drop out, but ultimately, they say, the movement will be stronger and, because of its wider scope, will appeal to more, not fewer, people. The tendency of this second group is to turn the movement into a political party.

Now, it is a great deal harder to launch a party than a movement, as American history amply demonstrates. Or, to make the same point in another way, it is all too easy to establish a very small political party, an association of activists who have the same position on almost everything. But a party that grows, losing something of its coherence yet retaining a common program—this is an extremely rare and difficult achievement. It may well be the "right" response even to very particular wrongs, rooted in sociological sophistication, reaching toward intellectual complexity and completion. But it requires too much from too many people— too much time, energy, money, above all too much commitment—to be politically viable. The movement, with all its necessary pretension, is more nearly possible. And victories can be won through single-issue campaigns. Indeed, it is hard to think of any other kind of victory that citizen activists have ever won. Winning turns out, of course, to be something less than they expected. The end of child labor, the achievement of women's suffrage, prohibition and its death, the end of this or that war: none of these planted the new Jerusalem. Nor, however, were they or will they be without significant effects, for good or ill.

Issues should be defined so that victories can be won. This doesn't mean that one should be able to imagine winning tomorrow. The question is not so much of time as of particularity and limit. It is always possible to describe one social problem so that it involves every other, so that its solution requires the solution of every other problem and the transformation of society as a whole. This is one of the major achievements of Marxist ideology. But it is also possible to describe one social problem as if it stands alone or sufficiently apart from other problems so that it can be solved without doing anything else or waiting for anything else to happen. Neither description is true, though it is possible that the first is more sophisticated.

Political activity anywhere in a society obviously produces adjustments, not necessarily transformations, everywhere. But the character and extent of these are almost impossible to predict. We make guesses and are usually wrong. In any case, action cannot and does not depend upon a true theory of social change. It requires a useful theory, or something less than a theory—a point of view, a set of opinions, an argument—that at least does not contradict whatever little we know to be true. And the most useful argument is one that imposes upon activists only one choice and only one fight at a time. They can always make further choices, join further fights, later on. Some members of the movement will want to plan ahead and should certainly do so, though not at the expense of the movement's immediate focus. That focus should almost certainly be on a single issue, an important issue, but simply stated: the vote, the war, the bomb. Activists and their spokesmen can safely exaggerate both the importance and the simplicity. Let victory bring its complications and disappointments.

5. SEARCHING FOR A CONSTITUENCY

A CONSTITUENCY is a social base, a sector of society (ethnic group, age group, economic class, or whatever) within which the movement finds sympathy and support, from which it recruits members, for which it claims to speak. But this constituency is not given, like that of a congressman or senator. It presumably has objective characteristics; it recognizably exists in the sense that men and women sharing those characteristics exist. But it is not organized; its members may not be conscious of the identity they share; nor does it act as a single body. Activists can try to turn it into a single body, a self-conscious whole, a collective force; or they can try to build such a body from among its members. Often they do the second, while pretending to do the first.

Finding a constituency is not always a problem. The constituency of the labor movement is the working class; organizers know exactly where to look for support (though they may look elsewhere as well). Generally, movements seeking to respond to injuries or injustices endured by particular groups of people plausibly direct themselves to those same groups. But sometimes such groups are thought to be incapable of defending themselves; someone must act on their behalf. And sometimes a movement is aimed at a policy thought to be unjust or immoral, but which is not injurious, or not obviously injurious, to any group of possible political actors (a foreign war, for example). In either of these last two cases, constituencies may be particularly hard to search out and put together. Yet the historical evidence is clear: the available people in such cases are largely middle class, and they come from fairly distinct sectors of the middle class: urban professional families, suburban housewives, students, and so on. I am not concerned here with efforts to explain the peculiar capacities of the middle class for moral indignation, nor with the level of education, leisure time, child-rearing practices, or ethnic history of its members. What is more important for our purposes are the special difficulties that middle-class activists have in dealing with their own people, their inevitable constituency.

The choice of action requires a break with the conventional world. Usually this is a break with the middle-class world, and the men and women who make it are eager to differentiate themselves from the people they have left behind.

Differentiation takes a great variety of forms, and many of these are harmless enough: small badges, self-awarded, for distinctive conduct. One form, however, is not harmless at all: the adoption of an ideology that focuses the new activist's hostility on his own past, his social or ethnic origins, his former friends and neighbors. This is appropriate for a revolutionary, perhaps, but it makes citizen activism a great deal harder than it need be. Activists do best if they begin by assuming that there are more people like them where they came from. They are wrong to think of themselves as unusual people, though they may well take pride in their resolution and energy. If they are in fact different in more fundamental ways, they are unlikely to be able to act effectively. *Begin where you are*—this is one of the central maxims of moral life, but in the life of a political movement it is often necessary to begin where you were.

This is especially important in the case of student activists. Their first constituency is the campus; their second is the world of their parents. They prefer often enough to go almost anywhere else (though they are unlikely to end up anywhere else). But there can be no doubt that they are most effective among the people they literally left behind, who are glad (mostly) to see them back. And they ought, whatever their preferences, to be as effective as they can.

I don't want to deny the need to reach or try to reach beyond immediately available constituencies. The efforts of middle-class activists to organize "in the community"—which usually means among working-class men and women—are sometimes worthwhile. For sometimes there are plausible signs that a working-class base can in fact be won or some substantial number of people recruited to the work of building their own base. But this is a foolish effort if there are no such signs, if the sole reason for not organizing elsewhere is the ideologically rooted belief that members of the middle class are different from "the people." In fact, of course, like everyone else, they are the salt of the earth.

6. GOING TO THE PEOPLE

IT'S NECESSARY to think twice before turning the movement loose on "the people." Efforts to reach beyond the middle class are so often ruined by the arrogance or condescension of the citizen activists involved. Their good intentions are transparent, but so, unhappily, is the assurance of superior wisdom that is the badge of their class. The truth is that the class barrier is painfully difficult to break through, and the difficulty is not reduced simply because activists agree on the importance of making the breach. This is not a boundary that one can just dash across. Indeed, the more sudden and seemingly uncalled for is the attempt, the more certain it is to fail. Failure can be seen clearly, I think, in the way workers look at students leafleting at a factory gate: "Who are you?" they seem to be saying. "Why are you here *today*? Where will you be *tomorrow*?" The effect is not much better when students spend a summer inside the factory. On the other side of the class line, a man is a stranger for a lot longer than two months. He is betrayed every time he opens his mouth, even if his rhetoric is as radical as it can be.

It makes more sense first to approach the leaders of whatever organizations are established among the people one is trying to reach: unions, churches, veterans' groups, community clubs. Many citizen activists explicitly assume that these leaders are not to be trusted. They are where they are, however, because people trust them, and unless some support can be found in their ranks, no other success can be expected. The notion, so common on the left, that workers must be organized "from below" is one of the clearest examples of the arrogance of the organizers: they assume they have some message to deliver that has never yet been thought of, let alone argued and championed, by leaders and would-be leaders within the working-class community itself. They are almost certainly wrong, as a more humble approach might well demonstrate.

Once contacts have been made, it is possible to think either of organizing a local branch or forming an alliance of some sort with groups that already exist. In either case, the actual work must be done by people established in the community. No serious political enterprise can be sustained for long by outsiders—though it is always possible to make a few converts and pretend to be leading a mass struggle. If local activists don't take charge, it's best to give up and begin again somewhere else. If they do take charge, they must be given their head. In time, the cause will be described in new accents; activity will take on a new style. It's all to the good if the movement comes to look very different in different parts of the country or even of the city.

When working among the poor, there is one thing that must never be forgotten: they have more immediate and pressing concerns than those of the movement. The worst kind of middle-class bias is the assumption that everyone else has, or ought to have, leisure, disinterest, and a passion for distant goods. In fact, for many people, a cause, even their own cause, is a luxury they can only occasionally afford. So a conventional politician who provides routine and necessary services easily wins a larger following than citizen activists with a program for Utopia, and he probably deserves the following he wins. His followers are rational men, not the victims (not, at least, in any simple sense) of oppression or "false consciousness." That is a reason, of course, for the movement staff to provide whatever services it can: day care, legal help, advice on available welfare programs. It is also a reason for seeking out conventional politicians and urging local activists to run for office. Among the poor, the movement cannot live on the cause alone; that is not, or not necessarily, a reason for giving up its single issue, but it does mean that it must ally itself with political groups and ambitious individuals who address themselves to other issues as well.

7. COALITIONS

WHEN POLITICAL activists are successful, even minimally successful, they not only add members to their own organizations; they also bring other organizations into action. The people they find are not facsimiles of themselves: they have, or many of them have, different interests and loyalties, different notions about appropriate channels. If they are to become active, they will probably do so only within their own groups. Some of these are established groups, their leaders suspicious of the movement, sensitive about their own prestige; some are as new as the movement itself, their members equally hopeful, but with some scheme or plan all their own. Some of them have only a peripheral interest in the cause; some are ready to take it on, full time, at least for a while. In any case, the movement must now consider the relative advantages of the many different kinds of cooperation, alliance, and coalition.

With all the good will in the world, cooperation is not easy, and in practice one must make do with considerably less good will than that. The crucial problem is that the different organizations compete with one another. They find themselves fighting for a limited supply of members, money, media coverage, and so on. To some extent, the single-issue movement can reduce the intensity of these fights and save itself a lot of trouble if it sticks to its own issue, promising, in effect, to go away once the cause has been won. Then it is less of a threat to ongoing groups, such as labor unions and political parties, whose leaders can now hope, if they cooperate, to inherit some of the people mobilized by the movement. But there is bound to be conflict, perhaps especially among groups with more or less similar or overlapping goals. They will disagree about strategies, aim at different constituencies (but compete in practice for the same core of activists), accuse one another of stupidity, fearfulness, and even betrayal.

For all this, alliances and coalitions are possible and necessary. The familiar maxim about strange bedfellows is, in fact, an injunction: it is the aim of political action, of day-to-day argument and maneuver, to get people into the same bed who never imagined they could take a peaceful walk together. But there are political (and moral) guidelines to be followed in establishing these peculiar intimacies, and citizen activists don't always succeed in plotting the appropriate course between puritanical fastidiousness and eager promiscuity. It is mostly a question of time and place, but also, as in moral life generally, of character. Some groups put themselves beyond the pale; sometimes it is necessary to say that with this or that organization, whose official policy requires, say, a defense of Nazi or Stalinist terror, no alliance of any sort is possible. This announcement is itself a political act, which lets people know something they have a right to know about the character of the movement. But when the questions at issue are of lesser moment, citizen activists ought never to make public display of their virtue. With ordinary corruption and opportunism, as with disagreeable opinions, they can deal—and they had better deal with them. The only question is on what terms.

The movement is best able to handle temporary alliances, planned with specific ends in view. Movement leaders should take the initiative in proposing particular actions, for which they can solicit particular kinds of help. They must expect, of course, to pay some price for the help they get and should always calculate in advance the various prices they are willing to pay for the gains they hope to make. Cooperating organizations will probably want to contact their own members, distribute their own literature, have a speaker on the platform, and so on. This is fine if, in return, they can turn out so many people, provide so many marshals, raise so much money; but it is a serious mistake if the "so many" and the "so much" are too little. Even with groups that can really help, negotiations are bound to be tricky. The movement is torn between the desire for unity and success and the (legitimate) fear of being misrepresented or even overwhelmed in a welter of dissident groups and programs, sectarian slogans, and irrelevant speeches. Obviously, decisions here must vary with cases, but it is worth warning against one very common form of blackmail.

Movement leaders are often afraid to break with groups to their left—even if small, undisciplined, and of little likely help—and so they are sometimes dragged into actions considerably more militant than those they had planned. The fear is not entirely senseless: far-left militants look more committed, ready to work longer hours and take greater risks; they evoke a naive kind of awe from many new activists. To say no to them appears either cowardly or half-hearted. Yet it is often necessary to say no—for three reasons which may serve as guidelines for coalition-making in general: to preserve the identity of the movement; to keep open the possibility of future alliances with the largest available groups;

and to continue to attract citizens presently uncommitted or advancing cautiously toward new political positions.

The important business of building long-term coalitions is probably best left to political professionals. It requires some delicacy and an almost endless capacity for compromise, and neither of these is (or ought to be) a strong point of citizen activists. Ongoing cooperation is only possible if the various movements with their different constituencies can be drawn into an organization that is greater than any of them and promises gains to all of them. The appropriate organization is the mass party, whether newly formed or old and established.

The promises are recognizably those of men seeking office. Citizen activists should aim at mobilizing their constituency so that this or that party will want to incorporate it and this or that office-seeker will want to make promises to it. Activists win most often by forcing their single issue into the platform of a major party, and then delivering their constituency at the polls. But they also lose, sometimes, by getting absorbed in party politics before they have mobilized a constituency of their own. Professional politicians prefer to bargain in the vaguest possible way with the largest possible groups. Movement activists must hold off until they can demand terms as specific as possible.

8. POLITICAL GEOGRAPHY

YOUNG activists can occasionally choose the communities where they want to work, but most citizens simply are where they are. And to some degree, at least, the problems they face and the choices they have to make depend on just where that is. Citizen politics is most interesting, most difficult, and often most bizarre in the great metropolitan centers and the university towns. Here activists need never fear that they will find themselves alone—not for five minutes at a time. Their numbers are sufficiently large to make for self-sustaining activity. They are less dependent on national offices, programs, and publicity than are their counterparts in small towns and suburbs. Much of their sustained activity, however, is factional feuding and sectarian intrigue. They are absorbed in one another. Occasionally it is possible—and it always looks possible, which is what makes politics so interesting— to mobilize large numbers of people in a single movement for a cause. This happens most readily in the context of a national campaign: only then are the stakes high enough to pull activists out of the local wars, or to pull new people in.

Politics is more serene in small towns and suburbs, where many of the problems I shall be discussing hardly arise. Often a fairly small group of people—the same group—enlist in every political movement. Wearing different hats, they defend different causes, and they rarely find themselves competing with anyone else. Coalition politics is easy in such a setting. But it may be a problem just to keep going and an even greater problem to persuade new people to join so visible and isolated a group. Here a sense of identification with an outside movement is absolutely crucial, and a national office can provide valuable services, making it possible for the local group to carry on a variety of activities month after month, year after year. The national office is itself sustained by such local groups, which somehow survive without ever expecting to. Militants from the metropolitan areas tend to be contemptuous of these local "do-gooders," but that is always a mistake. The "do-gooders" do good: they give the movement a presence and a base in times and places where the militants can't hope to supply either.

Whenever a nationwide campaign gains momentum, however, many of these groups will be overwhelmed, inundated by new members, unable to cope with the sudden end of a familiar and peaceful isolation. Some of the people they trained will hang on to provide continuity and leadership for whatever new organizations spring up. But power at such moments flows to the center (and out again in the form of itinerant organizers and campaign workers), or to the great cities where there are important victories to be won. If the campaign fails, the local groups will pick up the pieces and carry on.

The interconnections between local and national politics in the United States are extraordinarily complex. Though governmental decision-making is increasingly centralized and the media make it more and more difficult to sustain local activities that have no national significance, political power continues to be diffused, unevenly spread throughout the fifty states. This is especially so in political off-years—

three out of every four in electoral politics and more than that, probably, in the politics of most movements. People are trained for political action, loyalty is accumulated, organizations are slowly built up, all at the local level.

It is inevitable, therefore, that movements test the devotion and commitment of would-be leaders by their willingness to work at this level, to organize and agitate in relative obscurity, in small communities or urban neighborhoods. But it would be wrong to count too much on what activists commonly call "base-building," virtuous as it is, for there are fairly narrow limits to what can be accomplished without the spur and spectacle of life on the summit. Most causes must finally be won in Washington or on the way there. Whenever possible, then, the movement must project the image of a national struggle, even if nothing is happening except in San Francisco and New York. But its members must not be taken in by their own projections. The movement is a mirage unless it has, and at crucial moments can demonstrate that it has, a substantial following dug in here and here and here across the country. The national image sustains local activity, but only local activity can make the image real.

9. THREE ORGANIZATIONAL STRUCTURES

THE POLITICAL organizations of citizen politics can be divided roughly into three sorts, according to the location of power within them. It is possible to make moral claims about the superiority of one or another of the three, and such claims form a large part of movement debate. But I am inclined to think that each has its appropriate time and place. To argue about how *this* decision should be made makes sense and is often necessary. To argue about decision-making in general usually doesn't make sense and isn't necessary.

The most common organizational structure is that of the *front group*. Here power is firmly held by a central staff or by the group of men (sometimes a party or sect) that puts the staff together and pays its members. The wider membership has no power at all and rarely any active role to play. It is made up of people who allow themselves to be used. They lend their names and money, and sometimes their physical presence, to a cause. They presumably approve the cause, though they are sometimes deceived or deluded about its precise character. Or they trust some set of sponsors who have previously approved the cause, but who accept no responsibility for its day-to-day working out. Nor do the members (or more loosely, contributors, petition signers, demonstrators, and so forth) accept responsibility. They are not committed to any ongoing activity or involved in the internal politics of the organization. In the front group all politics is staff work.

The front group is correctly called an elitist structure. It tends steadily toward professional routine as staff members learn that from this sort of work they can make a living (more often, a living of sorts). It opens the way to manipulation and deceit whenever the staff decides that it can acquire a sufficiently large and impressive front only by disguising the nature of its activities. Nevertheless, citizens are not wrong to lend their names, make their contributions, attend rallies and demonstrations—sometimes—at the behest of this or that elite group. For there are important political victories most readily won by a competent staff that is relatively free to maneuver and at the same time to demonstrate mass support. I should add that such a staff is never entirely free; it is bound to the cause by the implicit threat of mass desertion.

Pressure politics is often organized on the model of the front group: the massive civil rights and anti-war demonstrations of the 1960's were essentially staff operations. In such cases, members of the central staff represent the interests or values of the participants to the rest of the world. They petition public officials, lobby in Congress, appeal to the country through the mass media, plan and publicize the march or rally itself. But the staff activists are by no means elected representatives. They begin, more likely, with interests and values of their own, then search out and put together the constituency for which they speak. The front group is ideal for the focusing and magnification of opinion. It is able to generate large-scale support, or the appearance of large-scale support, for this or that political position, precisely because such support does not require time-consuming or difficult work.

The work is done by the staff, which may also provide specialized services not otherwise available; thus the legal defense committee, publicizing some outrage of the judicial system in order to raise money for an appeal or to lobby for political intervention—while at the same time, perhaps, building sympathy for the politics of the defendants. The last of these is the least serious: the sympathy won is suitable only for instant display; it is unlikely to be deep-rooted or long-lasting. Staff work does not go very far in creating political consciousness, even when its other victories are impressive.

This is especially clear in election campaigns, which are run most often on the front-group model. The candidate is not chosen by the men and women who come to his aid; nor are strategic or even tactical decisions made by the volunteer workers. They do not determine (though they may affect) the candidate's position; they do not always know what that position is, or how serious or firm it is. They trust the candidate, and the work they do for him tends to intensify, even as it capitalizes on, that trust. Partly for this reason, it does not always intensify their commitment to the issue or program of the movement—unless they come into the campaign as members of movement groups structured very differently from the campaign organization itself.

The front group is not an instrument for sustained popular mobilization. Its staff can collect large numbers of signatures or even turn out thousands of people for an occasional demonstration or an election canvass. But ongoing activity requires a structure within which significant powers rest, at least formally, with the mass of activists. The second model, then, is *centralized democracy*, where the leadership is directly or indirectly elected by the members and responsible to them. Some degree of participation in internal politics by the members is here presupposed. The strength of the movement derives from the legitimacy that this participation confers on the center. The center can issue commands that are widely accepted; it can order a strike, demonstration, or election campaign with the assurance that men and women in large numbers will act together and do as they are told for as long as necessary. That, at any rate, is the ideal: a democratic movement can achieve an extraordinary discipline because it is founded on the consent of the disciplined (though also, sometimes, on class or ethnic solidarity).

It is rarely the case, however, that a large number of activists participate in the internal politics of the movement they support, and so the organization often assumes a dual character. The supporters are, in effect, a front, not, or not merely, for the central staff, but rather for a core of activists who rely on them for financial, moral, and occasionally physical support. Behind the front, there is cadre democracy, the self-government of the activists. This dual structure is one of the most useful for citizen politics, since it permits an easy movement between the wider following and the core. It is especially common among those local groups (in the anti-war movement, for example) that often provide the mass support necessary for national staff operations. Their cadres decide to participate, and call on their followers to participate, in demonstrations and elections they don't themselves plan or control. But they do plan and control their own participation and sustain a strong commitment to the cause. In such groups, both the demands that can be made on the followers and the freedom of the cadres are limited, but these limitations roughly fit the needs of citizen activism.

Centralized democracy without the dual structure is most suitable to parties, sects, and unions that need strong and stable leadership and sometimes make severe demands on their members. This is only possible if there is general agreement on policy and program. The democratic movement, in contrast to the democratic state, relies on a fairly tight consensus which most often takes the form of closely shared economic interests or a common ideology. Given this consensus, however, democratic controls on the leadership are often relaxed or even entirely surrendered, with results not very different from those that follow the same surrender in the state. Sects and unions are often formally democratic but in practice are run as autocracies. Then citizen activism is relevant only to the occasional rebellions that challenge the autocrats.

When no consensus at all exists, the best model for political activity is *federalism*. Here power rests with a number of centers, most often distributed geographically, each perhaps organized somewhat differently—as autocratic sects, cadre democracies, staff fronts, and so forth—all of them only loosely and informally coordinated. Every new proposal must be debated by each local. This project will be pressed by one, something quite different by another. Local option is the rule. The coordinating committee accumulates power only by convincing each local separately, and its power endures only for the length of whatever project is agreed upon. Federalism is a way of reflecting and coping with disagreements, but it has another feature often valued by citizen activists: it increases the number of people involved in decision-making; it decreases the possibilities of elitist manipulation (or, it multiplies and disperses the elite groups).

Unless there are significant victories to be won at the

local level, federalism is the least effective pattern for political action. Local option deprives the national leadership of both authority and initiative; it virtually precludes negotiation or alliance with other political forces; it makes even short-term planning extremely difficult. It is probably best seen as an early stage in the development of citizen politics, when new groups are springing up and no "government" has yet emerged. But it often survives for a long time, even after many activists have despaired of its effectiveness, simply because no one can figure out how to weld together or overcome the local power centers.

If the original group of activists hopes to retain control of the growing movement, they obviously cannot choose a federal structure. They may simply maintain the façade they first raised and work out of an office behind it, or they may try to win mass support as a reward for their initiative. The last of these is the most interesting, since the activists will certainly encounter opposition. Conflict is inherent in a democratic organization. This is not necessarily divisive; it can have energizing effects, stimulating internal debate, generating a kind of competition in effectiveness. But it also raises, often in dramatic fashion, the question of leadership. For the best political organization may turn out to be not the one that is best organized but the one that is most ably run.

10. LEADERS

A SURPRISINGLY large number of people do not want political power. They have no eagerness for command, no thrusting willfulness. They want to do the right thing; they also want someone to tell them what the right thing is. So it is one of the major difficulties of a new movement that leaders cannot easily be recruited from among its rank and file. The individuals who do put themselves forward tend to have previous political experience and holdover commitments, personal or ideological, that are sometimes incompatible with the proclaimed aims of the movement. Would-be leaders may well discover in citizen activism not a movement for a cause but a vehicle for their own ambitions. Two sorts of people, above all, need to be considered here: disgruntled professionals and sectarian militants. Both sorts are or can be useful to the movement, but they are also predatory on the movement, and it is a mistake to allow either to displace whatever amateur leadership can be discovered or produced, however reluctant and inexperienced the amateurs are.

Politicians out of office are bound to see in any citizens' movement an opportunity for themselves. Some of them will commit themselves to the cause, with more or less fervor, and seek to absorb the activists into their own campaign organization. Within the movement, such commitments are often regarded with skepticism: why wasn't this or that professional politician committed before? (There is an obvious rejoinder: why weren't the citizens active before?) Perhaps the skepticism is justified, but the availability of opposition professionals is also an opportunity for the activists. Here is their crucial access point to the political system. What is necessary now is that the citizens find a way of providing the support the professionals need in their pursuit of office without ceasing to provide the stimulus and pressure they also need. In order to do this, the movement and the candidacy should probably remain distinct, even while members of the movement turn themselves into campaign cohorts for the candidate. There are two reasons for stressing this distinction. First, the candidate is unlikely to be willing to lead the movement as an independent force, either because he believes he must reach beyond its membership or, as in the case of Senator McCarthy in 1968, because his whole career and his sense of himself preclude movement politics. Second, the movement must plan on surviving November, and it is not always in the interests of the candidate that it do so. It's necessary, then, to recognize the candidate as a national (or local) leader while still supporting a separate movement leadership.

Sectarian militants sense a different sort of opportunity in the new movement: a chance to educate and recruit, to move outside the narrow circles of their own routine activity. They may also, of course, be committed quite straightforwardly to the cause, but the cause, whatever it is, will have resonances in their minds very different from those it has for other activists. Insofar as the militants assume positions of leadership—as they will do, for they are often extraordinarily diligent in everyday politics—they will seek to fix the movement within the structure of their own ideological program. In their hands, citizen activism can be turned into a front for the sectarian band or a channel through which committed individuals are directed into the world of sect life. And then bewildered citizens will flee the movement, retreating nervously before the ideological intensity and the long-term planning of the militants. In a very strict sense, sects are parasitic on movements; ideological militants feed on indignant citizens.

But the militants can also provide important services to citizen activists, and since the relation between the two can't be avoided, just as the relation of professionals and amateurs can't be avoided, it must be worked out so as to permit the survival and growth of whatever political activity citizens manage to launch. Professionals and militants seek to exploit the movement; the movement must find ways to exploit them. It must use the time, energy, competence, and zeal of the militants for its own legitimate purposes without succumbing to their ideology. On this or that project, they will work feverishly, harder than anyone else, and certainly they should be encouraged to do so. But they must also be denied what they will surely regard as the just rewards of their toil. This can only be done by an "indigenous" leadership confident of its own purposes, freed from the delusions of instant victory (which opens it to the professionals) and ultimate redemption (which opens it to the sectarians). No great capacity for organizational intrigue is necessary here. Leaders with a solid base, in touch with their constituency, need only a little resolution and ordinary stubbornness to win out.

Citizen activism has its own time scale, and its leaders must be attuned to the implicit rhythms of less than total commitment, part-time work, and (relatively) short-term goals. But here I come back to the original difficulty: part-time and short-term activists do not seek leadership positions, and tend not to make self-confident leaders even when they are chosen by their comrades. They must nevertheless be chosen and given what support they need. I cannot think of anything more important to the success of citizen politics (especially on the local level) than the cultivation of citizen leaders. Capable men and women are available. They appear in the midst of every strike, demonstration, and election campaign. They assume responsibilities, they cope with crises. They disappear, however, as soon as the full-time politicians, professional or sectarian, arrive on the scene and confidently start telling everybody what to do.

But those leaders know best what to do who know the people who have to do it. And that is why it is worth looking hard for ways to open political life to talented activists who have other lives to live. These same people must be encouraged to hang on when challenged and enabled to move out of their own local into the national office—and back again—when they are ready. One way to help them I will take up immediately: that is, to finance their activity so that they need neither commit themselves (and their families) to poverty nor seek out professional status and rewards.

11. RAISING AND SPENDING MONEY

THE EASIEST way to get money is to ask for it. There are a variety of people to ask: wealthy and politically serious men and women who have to be convinced that this project and not that one deserves support; promoters and angels for whom politics is another kind of theater—they want only to be assured of fashionability and success; guilty nonparticipants who might like to march and demonstrate except for all the reasons they have for not doing so; and, finally, marchers and demonstrators themselves, some of whom, at least, can pay as they go. The first two groups must be approached in person; the others through the media and the mails. Activists don't often make good beggars, and here (elsewhere too) they should not hesitate to get professional help—and to pay for it.

But the best way to get money is to earn it (or some of it, since there is no way to avoid begging) through the conventional fund-raising activities of nonpolitical organizations. It is not puritanism, or not that alone, that leads me to insist upon the value of earning money. Fund-raising is an important activity because it enables large numbers of people to express their support for the movement in ways that also utilize their everyday competence and give them something important to do. Among the most demoralizing features of political life are the long spells of inaction, the time spent standing around or wasted in desultory debate and factional infighting. Fund-raising is both time-consuming and useful. Many people are accustomed to it and do it well; and the sense of a job to be done that can be done is a crucial factor in generating loyalty to the cause and self-confidence in the activists. So a successful auction, book fair, or bake sale is a (minor) triumph for peace, integration, women's rights, socialism, or whatever: so many people are doing something and not merely waiting for the Revolution. Political action has, I suppose, its moments of glory, but activists must learn to serve proudly the gods of the commonplace.

The ways in which money is earned (and spent) affect also the constitutional balance of the movement. Internal democracy is fostered when money is earned by the members, even more so when it is initially accumulated by local branches. Members and locals are more likely then to insist on a say in spending it, and the center will be more sensitive to their opinions. (This is less likely when the members merely pay dues to the center, especially if that payment has become routine in one way or another.) Private contributors obviously place power in the same hands they put the money in. They help to build strong staffs or central committees. The causal connection works the other way too: men who aspire to form a strong central committee must search for financial backing.

However it is accumulated, the distribution of money is certain to be a major focus of political controversy. Perhaps the most crucial argument in new parties and movements, and one I want to dwell on, is whether or not to pay campaign workers. Freely given time and energy are an absolute prerequisite of citizen politics; without that nothing is possible, and there is great pressure to make do with that alone, or, at most, to pay a bare subsistence to those activists who require it. After all, how can one hire a man's enthusiasm? And how can he charge the movement for doing what is (presumably) every citizen's duty? Yet there are two problems with unpaid or barely paid activists that must be faced if structure and leadership are to be provided for any ongoing work. First, payment is a crucial connection to the center. A man who takes money is also likely to take orders. However much must be said for the independent activist whose moral commitment is his only connection to the movement, it remains true that his cooperation and obedience cannot be guaranteed. It is never certain that he is committed to these particular leaders or to this particular program (rather than to the cause in general). That is his strength, but sometimes the movement's weakness. At certain key moments, in certain key positions, one simply needs people who will do as they are told. Of course, there are ties other than the moral bond and the cash nexus (friendship is perhaps the most important in informal groups, collective discipline in highly organized parties), but mostly we take pledges and distribute money, and the possible utility of the second should not be overlooked.

The second problem relates to the class and age of the activists. Unpaid work comes most often from the young and the well-to-do. The prototypical activist is the upper-class student who often makes politics seem, like romantic love, a matter of world enough and time. His devotion is profound, his energy extraordinary, and, most important of all, his days are free. Clearly, he will provide much of the manpower necessary for any ongoing activity. But he cannot provide a stable base for the movement; he is without roots in any particular community. Adults must be brought in, not merely as patrons and supporters but as workers. This requires that work schedules be adjusted so as to permit part-time participation. It also requires that some people be paid and even that they be paid fairly well so that they can (temporarily) give up their regular jobs and still support their families. The movement must make its peace with a certain amount of semi-professionalism since so many adults can't afford to be amateurs in the literal sense. I should stress that they often can't afford amateur status in other ways too. The movement's readiness to pay them is a sign of the value it places on their work, a sign they might not be willing to relinquish even if they were financially able to do without the money. Activists may disapprove of the need for such signs, but they are not acting in the society they hope to create. They are acting in this one and alongside its inhabitants with their peculiar needs. There is an alternative to all this, however, that should be discussed separately: the exploitation of the housewife, as common in the movement as in society at large.

12. THE WOMAN QUESTION

PROFESSIONAL politics is overwhelmingly a man's world. In citizen politics, women play a much larger part. Indeed, they constitute a majority of the adult participants in many activities. Young activists, struggling to get something started "in the community," find women reachable in ways that men on the job are not (to them); and women with families and without jobs in fact have time to spare for politics—just as they have time to spare for the church, the PTA, hospital aid, and so on. Politics is not so different from these, though it is sometimes more important. So women are drawn in; they do important work and work at which they are often highly experienced. But they only rarely emerge as leaders, and they rarely make the weight of their experience and participation felt when crucial decisions are being made.

The reasons for this don't have much to do with citizen politics in particular. The subordination of women, especially older women, in the new party or movement is only one more example of their position in the old society. The conventional activities that women most readily take up in the movement are those that are most seriously underpaid out of it. And the part-time work that is easiest for women with children is everywhere undervalued, by no means peculiarly so in the movement. Yet in the movement as out of it, women defer to men—to young activists, political old hands, semi-professionals, and part-time leaders who meet, argue, bargain, and hand down decisions. Even when women play key managerial roles in citizen politics, they are usually excluded from the boards of directors and steering committees which assume ultimate responsibility for movement projects. Sometimes this exclusion has a political excuse; often, it has to be said, the women involved do not resist. Unsure of their political roles, nervous about their family commitments, lacking in self-confidence, they allow themselves to become the common laborers of the movement.

There are any number of objections to be made to this situation, and the most important I leave to the women themselves. I only want to point out one consequence of their subordination for citizen politics, that is, the ephemeral character of so many amateur movements. This is caused at least partly by the way in which power in these movements gravitates toward people who are marginal to any particular local community and away from people—a very large number of them women—who have established themselves where they are and assumed local responsibilities.

It is important to point out the contrast here with established political parties and labor unions which are essentially associations of adult males, rooted in their communities, supplemented and sometimes strengthened by Ladies Auxiliaries. Citizen politics can rarely take that form, since so many men are committed elsewhere. More important, it shouldn't take that form since one of its characteristic claims is to mobilize people who have been previously passive, unheard within the system. Women are one of its key constituencies, and their degradation is its especial loss. The failure of women to assume leadership positions or to participate fully in decision-making often leaves the new party or movement rootless, the ideological tool and sometimes the plaything of marginal men.

13. MEETINGS

A CHURCH basement with cinder-block walls and linoleum floor, rows of uncomfortable metal chairs, a hundred or so people of all ages: here is a political meeting. Perhaps the people are leaders or representatives of local groups, perhaps they are simply members. I assume that they are meeting to make policy decisions and that they have met before. Typically, they have met too often before, and this meeting goes on too long. Too many people speak; the chairman flounders; older participants start to leave, fleeing homeward; no clear decisions are reached; another meeting is called for next Tuesday.

The tendency of citizen politics is toward democracy of expression, an equalitarianism of the vocal chords, which is wonderfully exhilarating—a week, a month ago, these were *silent* men and women—until it becomes exhausting and tedious. Often the political assemblies of citizen activists turn into what early Protestants called "experience meetings," where one participant after another testifies to his motives for joining the movement. Almost everyone wants a chance, has a story to tell that is or may be relevant to the issue at hand. And then to the testimonies are added the ideological explanations of three or four political old hands, fiercely antagonistic to one another, demanding equal time. Somehow pressing issues are not resolved, though much that is

49

said is interesting, educational, even exciting. And the following Tuesday fewer people come, above all, fewer older people, married people, mothers, men and women with full-time jobs. Expressive democracy is perfectly compatible with autocratic decision-making. In fact, autocrats have a vested interest in meetings of this sort.

If significant decisions are to be reached at meetings, there are a number of simple rules to follow. It may not be so simple to follow them: the question of how decisions are best made inevitably gets tangled up with the question of which decisions are best to make. Nevertheless, I think it is almost always better to try to get the best decision out of a relatively large meeting than to exhaust and depress the people who come to meetings and then make the decision alone or with a small group of allies. Better the church basement than the living room, as soon as there is a choice. But this requires, first, that meetings be infrequent and, second, that they be managed.

The chairman must be someone capable of taking charge: cutting off irrelevant speeches, pressing the central issues, insisting on a vote before people start for home. Since the infrequency of meetings is possible only if subgroups get together in the intervals, committees appointed by the chairman and factions self-assembled from among like-minded activists must arrive at each meeting with proposals to make and opinions to defend. The chairman should know what these proposals and opinions are and who is going to present them, so that he can call on speakers in some plausible order. If he isn't in touch before the meeting, he won't be in control at the meeting. The chairman should never be surprised—which is not to say that he should always be successful in getting what he wants.

Running a meeting is often confused with manipulating it. That's not a silly confusion. Manipulating a meeting means running it with some purpose in mind beyond merely running it well. Chairmen often have such purposes in mind. That's why it is important to insist that they stick to some set of rules. A rough version of parliamentary procedure is probably best, but virtually any rules will serve, so long as they set limits to what chairmen (and others) can do.

It is often argued by new activists that no such rules are necessary among friends and comrades, but the idea of the ruleless meeting is, I'm afraid, hopelessly misconceived. It rests on the belief that agreements can be reached through uncontrolled and unlimited discussion if only the "spirit" of the meeting is sufficiently warm. But it generally isn't sufficiently warm, and most people, in any case, won't sit through the endless talk. When meetings are not run according to rules, their manipulation becomes more, not less, important—and much harder to detect. Formally shapeless discussion provides an absolutely open field for the manipulative craft of a few people. The crucial feature of orderly procedures is that they identify such people as responsible agents: the chairman himself, the mover of this or that motion, and so on. Meetings can be manipulated from the back row, but run well (and honestly) only from the front.

There are eighteen ways of manipulating a meeting, and it is best if there are eighteen groups, no less, trying to be manipulative, struggling to make their proposals sound like what everybody (really) wants. Then none of them is likely to have things all its own way. One of the problems of citizen politics is that most new activists come to meetings not knowing what they want to accomplish before they leave. Then they are in the hands of the others—professionals, militants, faction-men, and committeemen—who know exactly what they want. This difficulty can only be resolved over time, by making meetings as accessible, and procedures as transparent, as possible.

Meetings should be spaced so that part-time activists don't feel that the costs of attendance are prohibitive. They should never last so long that people with families or jobs feel that they have to leave. The rules should be clear, relatively simple, widely known. A great deal of work should be done by sub-groups meeting at the convenience of their members. These are seemingly easy matters, but they often involve consider-able resistance to the pressures of activists with time to spare. Here are dangerous men, who feel that the movement needs their fullest devotion (it may need that) and who express that devotion by insisting, eagerly, ruthlessly, stubbornly, on one interminable meeting after another.

The central purpose of meetings is to involve the largest possible number of people in decision-making. The front group, therefore, can dispense with meetings almost entirely. It requires only rallies, which serve quite different purposes: ideological development, moral catharsis, the quickening of enthusiasm and solidarity. A good meeting can serve these purposes too, but it must do two other things as well: distribute power and impose responsibility. Unless it does them both successfully, the movement belongs to its leaders or to its staff.

14. THE OFFICE STAFF

A MOVEMENT office isn't all that different from any other office; there isn't much to say about it. But a certain amount of political power is necessarily lodged there, and it is worth worrying about its precise lodging place. The office staff will consist mostly of part-time people, moving in and out, doing routine work. They will not find it easy to exercise much influence; they may not even try to do so, unless they are prompted. A number of full-time people will make day-to-day decisions, following loosely or strictly the policy directives of the central leadership and the mass meeting—loosely if the leaders stay away, closely if they come around. A leader who can run a meeting but can't or doesn't bother to make his presence felt in the office is unlikely to lead very effectively. The danger here is that the office may be "seized" by people who don't have the confidence of the mass meeting, but who don't need it because the leadership, knowingly or not, fronts for them. This is especially likely in a movement of part-time activists and part-time leaders. Perhaps a front group is appropriate to whatever activity they are all engaged in, but it isn't always appropriate, and the leaders (on behalf of the members) should be able to control the office if they choose to.

Staff power is sometimes described as a special kind of democracy: the necessary product of the right that people have to control the work they do. But the staff works *for* the movement and is responsible to it. Its members go to meetings like everyone else, probably more regularly, and, given an atmosphere of trust and good will, their position and knowledge will make them more influential than less active members can possibly be. The only other reward they can ask for the extra work they do is to be paid for it.

One last point: the records kept in the office—mailing lists, financial reports, correspondence—are very important, necessary if political work is to be sustained for any length of time or renewed after some temporary setback. Someone should look after them, and activists should insist that they are in fact looked after by people they know and trust.

15. PERSONAL RELATIONS IN THE MOVEMENT

IT IS A mistake to join the movement in search of love. Intimacy is neither a necessary nor a common feature of political life. The heightened emotions of collective action are peculiarly impersonal: they bring the individual into touch with too many other people to bring him into close touch with anyone in particular. Not love, but *amour social*, camaraderie, solidarity, are the unifying passions of the movement. And they are only sometimes intense and vivid passions. Most often, the size of the movement, the range of activities carried on by its members, the ever-present disagreements about strategy and tactics, the competition for leadership, the need to keep things together—all these tend to preclude the expression of strong feelings for particular people. (Strong feelings for abstract ideas are more commonly expressed.) Political association is the art of keeping one's distance: too close is a danger and a distraction; too far is a loss of control and influence.

Personal ties do exist within the movement, and sometimes they produce a kind of subpolitics that stands in various degrees of tension with the general commitment of activists to their cause. I am thinking especially of the subpolitics of the coterie and the entourage. A coterie is a sect without an ideology, a band of friends more deeply involved with one another than with the movement itself, more trusting of one another than of anyone else. Its members can be a divisive force (without ever intending division) simply because they intensify and exacerbate everyone's personal sensibilities. Ideally, I suppose, activists should leave at home their native alertness to slurs and snubs and heighten instead their sensitivity to the nuances of political disagreement. In practice, the two are mixed, held in some sort of rough balance. The danger of the coterie is that it tips the balance away from public disputes toward private intrigue. This is especially dangerous if the leadership itself is a band of friends, for many activists are sure to resent their exclusion who would not do so if they thought they were being excluded for political rather than personal reasons. Intelligent leaders will associate themselves with people who are not their friends, even with people they do not like.

An entourage is a band of people who wait upon a leader (and generally keep him from associating with anyone who is not an active admirer). Members of the entourage are loyal to the leader, not at all to one another. Now loyalty to a leader is one of the most profound and tenacious of political emotions, but it is relatively rare, perhaps refreshingly rare, in the world of citizen politics where leaders have all too little standing with their followers. Occasionally a man or woman who has been in trouble with the authorities, stood trial, or endured imprisonment will win a special kind of following. But that is not very dependable, particularly if a number of persons have stood trial and endured imprisonment.

The entourage appears most often when some individual who is powerful in the outside world joins the movement, bringing his admirers with him. This sort of thing can cause problems not only because it ruptures the easy familiarity and camaraderie of the movement, but also because it stands in the way of a cool assessment of the actual possibilities of power and personality in political life. These possibilities are generally greater than citizen activists are willing to admit, especially when confronted by a leader and his entourage. Once again, it is a question of keeping one's distance. Great Men have a part to play, but it is not a good idea to have their favorites write the script.

If love is uncommon in political life, hatred is common enough, and it takes getting used to. One of the hardest things for new activists to learn is that politics involves them constantly in antagonistic relations with other people. A few of them turn out to enjoy such relations, but most do not. Yet the movement can offer only modest support to members experiencing for the first time the anger and hostility of political opponents. Its leaders and publicists can explain how it is that political disagreements are so deeply rooted, social and economic interests so fundamentally opposed. Other members can offer their understanding and solidarity. But too much should not be expected. Ultimately one draws on personal resources to cope with the hatred of another man or woman. Solidarity is a political tie, subject to political strains. It may not outlast the first serious argument over strategy and tactics. The movement itself is an arena of conflict and antagonism. Commitment and camaraderie most often mute the everyday disagreements. But sometimes they fail, and then the internal polemics and power struggles can be intense and bitter—especially so, perhaps, for those members who had dreamed of unity and devotion.

16. QUACKERY AND INEXPERIENCE

IT IS JUST possible that there is a higher proportion of fools in the movement (any movement) than in the general population. Certainly that is the way things look to the conventional eye. Marginal politics attracts marginal people who are ill at ease, resentful, graceless, unhappy, or frightened in the everyday world. They experience the perversions of common sense, perhaps in a profound way; foolishness, so to speak, is thrust upon them. The movement liberates them, or leads them to think they are liberated, and so it becomes an arena within which their repressed discontents are acted out, their secret nostrums revealed, often in naive and extravagant ways. They are set free to dress, talk, live in unconventional styles that may or may not be the styles of the future, but which serve now as expressions of hostility toward the present. A kind of diffuse outrage plagues the movement, a surplus of pent-up emotional energy which is equally dangerous when it floats freely and when it fixes upon a single theory of the world's ills. There is no easy remedy for all this. A solid organization and a lot of hard work can go some way toward transforming into disciplined indignation the latent hysteria that most political systems only repress and exploit. But until that transformation occurs, activists must suffer fools, if not gladly, at least patiently. They are all in rebellion against what passes for commonsense politics, and it is not easy (so they will learn) to sustain that rebellion without sometimes appearing senseless.

Inexperience is somewhat less of a problem, for politics is less an acquired skill than the professionals pretend. I don't mean that there isn't a lot to learn; there is. And there are moments, too, when professional advice can be very helpful. But the professionals make disastrous mistakes, and they seem to make them randomly. New activists sometimes find themselves in that enviable position best described by saying: they can hardly do worse than has been done. Or, if worse is always possible, so is better. It happens often that the chances of political life favor the amateur: because he tries new tactics, takes greater risks, works feverishly hard, conveys a sharp sense of excitement and urgency, exploits the enormous and perennial appeal of innocence. The last of these is the most interesting. I suppose inexperience is the easiest kind of innocence; it has the attraction of the *gauche* rather than the pure. But there is method in the *gaucherie;* it is an important vehicle for the expression of moral feelings.

So long as the outrage of the activists is not hysterical or their appearance outlandish, the combination of *gaucherie* and righteousness makes a powerful political force. There is a strong popular presumption in favor of the inexperience of a moral man and also of the morality of an inexperienced man. This is the secret of the anti-political (anti-professional) campaign—one of the most successful kinds of politics.

The difficulties of inexperience are most apparent when new activists absorb their first setback, or when they first realize that much of the work they have to do is unexciting, not all that different from the routines of conventional politics. It's the settling into the movement that is hard—the first campaign is delightful—and it is made much harder if one's fellow activists are struggling to sustain the drama of their own earliest encounters. They can do this for a while at least, largely by the frenetic way they talk to one another and to outsiders. And then the movement takes on a tense and heated quality that does not prepare its members even for the relatively short-term politics of citizen activism.

New activists eagerly play parts in each other's fantasies and imagine themselves involved in important battles for the cause. The real battles come as a shock. The dull, continuous work, the necessary discipline, the minor setbacks and disappointments, the indifference or hostility of most of the world, the need to come back tomorrow and do again whatever was done today: these are the initiatory experiences of political life. Until a significant number of citizens have survived them, there is no real movement at all, but only an inchoate band of discontented men and women ready for an adventure that may or may not have much to do with the cause they espouse.

The tactical mistakes of inexperienced activists are endless and unimportant. At any rate, they don't distinguish citizen politics from any other kind. One learns and recovers, or not. The real failures of new activists tend to be gross; they are failures of nerve and endurance, marked by sudden defections, wild talk, personal indulgence, dangerous adventures. Against all these the movement must struggle almost as energetically as against whatever feature of the old society it is opposing. But its leaders must never forget that the people who act out these failures are their own people, their only hope for success. They cannot dissolve the mass of activists and find another.

17. TELLING THE TRUTH

TALKING is the most common form of political activity. Often people join the new party or movement eager to "do something" and then are frustrated and confused to find themselves mostly talking—to one another. They have to talk to one another in order to decide what to do, and whatever they decide is certain to involve talking with other people. Despite the skepticism they come to express—*only* talk, *mere* words—all this does have effects, even significant effects. I don't think that anyone who has ever attended a meeting can doubt that people are indeed swayed by skillful speech. They are also swayed, though probably in smaller numbers, by skillful writing. It makes sense, then, to try to say something about skill with words, though I cannot offer a treatise on rhetoric. I want to focus instead on the problem of truthfulness in political speech, a perennial issue and one especially pressing in the movement, which is so often racked by debates between honest zealots and idiot Machiavellians. Two questions are crucial: How complex (or simple) should political arguments be? How straightforward (or evasive) should political speakers and writers be?

Once a man has taken a stand on a particular issue, he is tempted to take a stand on every issue. One thing leads to another; everything interconnects. He is pressed toward a total ideological position; he yearns for intellectual coherence, unity, completion. Now a total view of political life, if it is radical and new, requires a fairly elaborate language, a complex jargon with its own intellectual and idiomatic conventions. But it can often be summed up and presented, precisely because of its total character, with breathtaking simplicity. It can be expressed politically, at meetings, marches, and demonstrations, in those stark slogans whose loud reiteration is a hallmark of sectarian militancy and a hostile act against the unbelieving world. If the unbelievers turn away, as they naturally do, this does not mean that they don't have slogans of their own. Professional politicians fully understand the value of reiteration, though they can afford to be quieter than the militants. Their catchwords also reflect total views, not necessarily views recently worked out or even thought about, but similar in the range of issues they touch upon to those of the most ambitious sectarian ideologist. And these conventional ideologies, which don't require a new jargon, but are routine and automatic in common speech, are believed, or at any rate accepted, by vast numbers of people.

When citizen activists break with some conventional view, they generally do so, or think they do so, for simple reasons. But as they involve themselves in political argument, they discover that one convention fits (roughly) with another. They are committed to more rethinking and worrying than they had anticipated. This is what makes so many of them suddenly available to anyone with a new ideology: they are prey for the militants. But the position of new activists is unstable in a much more important way. A few reassuring words from some politician in power may bring them quickly back to the old conventions and routines. So it is vitally important that those activists capable of speaking and writing undertake to explain to the others their new position.

They have a lot of explaining to do. They need to offer reasons for their move into what is actually a kind of limbo. Not one reason, but lists of reasons, for they are likely to be speaking to people of very different sorts from very different backgrounds. They cannot speak either in systems or in slogans. I think there is an important sense in which citizen politics, by its very character, is opposed to total ideologies in both their routine and their radical manifestations. Its participants are drawn away from conventional politics but remain uncommitted as a group to any single alternative. Their unity is partial and probably temporary, and their spokesmen should not pretend that it is anything else. They have to make arguments without claiming that the arguments they make are linked together in some complex whole. As for their style, it is not so much intellectual brilliance or any sort of verbal legerdemain that is necessary as what used to be called plain speech: simple language, a quiet tone, an air of calm, a slow pace. All this is reassuring, and none of it, I should add, is incompatible with anger. The worst thing of all is hysteria, in some ways the most sincere response to political crisis, but the most disturbing and frightening to uncommitted onlookers.

The great advantage that activists have is that they speak the same language as other citizens. They should continue to do so, elaborating the conventional catchwords in new ways, for example, rather than initiating one another into strange ideological idioms. They should challenge one convention at a time, as it becomes necessary, and in any given period as few as possible. Above all, they should establish priorities and stick to them: if the movement hopes to persuade people to oppose the war, for example, its members should not make radical pronouncements about sex or drugs or any other fashionable and exciting issue that catches their eye.

But this course of action may well seem less than honest to many citizen activists and, what is more important, to some of the most articulate among them. They have begun, perhaps, to rethink all their political beliefs; they see or think they see that this particular action has consequences throughout the political system; it must or it should lead to further action. They sense a more general crisis, once they have cut their ties and begun to act, than they ever did before. They are tempted by one or another radical ideology. And they want to tell all, to describe with the utmost sincerity their own evolving position. They should do this if they like within the movement, certainly among the core of activists, even though most of their speculations about the future, like everyone else's, will turn out to be wrong.

But it is another kind of mistake to carry this sort of thing over into public argument. Most citizens will take their first step beyond the conventions only if they think they have an option (as in fact they generally do) about the second step. So the discontent out of which the movement grows needs to be pointed and made precise, and proposed actions need to be described in concrete and limited terms. Neither of these purposes are served by personal descriptions of social crisis or by loose talk, however honest, about the imminent fall of established systems. Sometimes it makes sense to suggest connections between *this* issue and some other, but often not. Sometimes it is useful to sketch out complex aspirations and distant goals, often only to point to near victories. These are political, not personal, decisions, and they depend most of all on a judgment as to the requirements of a particular constituency. I don't mean that activists should lie, only that they should sometimes be silent. Their confessional tendencies especially need to be restrained. Political activity is not a judicial proceeding; activists should tell the truth, but not necessarily the whole of it at every moment.

18. SYMBOLS

IT'S NOT only what we say that is important in politics, but how we look. Visual impacts are sometimes crucial; our appearances signify; they convey meanings to other people. And so it is always necessary for activists to ask: What does this gesture, insignia, costume, flag, mean *to them*? Symbols can be chosen, of course, that mean nothing, to which meanings have to be given—like the bisected circle with an inverted V that has symbolized the peace movement since the 1950's. I don't know what associations that had for its originators; for most of the rest of us, it had none at all. This blankness is probably an advantage: everyone attributes his own significance; no one is turned away.

The clenched fist is a symbol of an exactly opposite sort. It has overwhelming historical associations and in any case carries an immediate and unmistakable meaning. It conveys a sense of aggressiveness and violence which is sometimes intended, but often not, by those who make the gesture. Gestures are like rhetoric: the speaker allows himself to exaggerate, but many members of the audience take him at his word.

Activists rarely reckon with the literal-mindedness of the people in front of whom they act. They think they will be accorded the liberties of the stage even when they are in the streets. Thus obscenity came to be used among some citizen activists at the same time as it came to be used in the theater. But the two uses have very different effects. In the theater, obscenity conveys a shock, a thrill, a sense of danger and extremity (for a little while). But the words themselves don't carry for the audience their literal meaning. In political encounters they do; they express real insult and hostility, and they invite an immediate response which ought never to come as a surprise. The abuse of the flag, as a symbol of political protest, similarly has literal meanings. It is an invitation to patriotic outrage, and that is even worse than personal outrage.

In general, it is a mistake to take one's symbols from the avant-garde culture of the time. To do so inevitably turns political action into an elite performance and a kind of esoteric communication. Similarly, it's a mistake for activists to imitate the life styles of Bohemia—unless it is their primary object to organize Bohemians. Those styles have associations for other people that have or should have nothing to do with movement politics. They represent so much excess weight, and the burdens of dissent are heavy enough. Symbols should lighten the weight, attract new people, make winning easier not harder: V-for-victory is fine.

19. THE MASS MEDIA

THE PRESENTATION of the movement in everyday life does not, at first, appear to be a major problem. When an individual activist canvasses up and down a street, standing in doorways, sitting in living rooms, talking, he is more or less in control of the image he presents. The central committee that directs the canvassing or organizes a demonstration is more or less in control of the immediate impact of those activities. But as soon as a journalist or a cameraman appears on the scene, all such control is lost.

What the media do with the movement is so erratic that it is very difficult to detect a pattern or work out a strategy. Sometimes they pick up a campaign that is struggling along with no great success in sight and publicize it to the nation, vastly increasing its size and scope. Here is the dream of many little bands of activists: suddenly to be made important. More often, the media only glance at citizen politics and reflect the judgment of the professionals as to its significance. Then activists think they find a "consistent ideological bias" in newspaper and television coverage, and they attribute to this bias the fact that they are being ignored. I suspect they are wrong (though not always). The consistent bias of the news media is toward novelty and excitement, not toward right, left, or center. Of course, what is new today depends on what was news yesterday. So if one campaign is extensively covered, the next may not be covered at all; and after a period of neglect, an activity fitfully sustained for some time will abruptly be discovered. One does not choose; one is chosen.

Given the essentially arbitrary quality of media coverage, there is still some room for maneuver. Local newspapers are especially open: activists able to grind out copy can get almost as much coverage as they want. And it does matter, though it is hard to say how much, that press releases be well written, news conferences properly staged, celebrities and Great Men intelligently exploited. Political action has or can have a dramatic quality which activists should not deny or repress. Nor is it shameful to seek out professional help with such things, so long as the professionals are told that they must take the movement as it is, not try to make it more presentable. (Perhaps the movement *should* be made more presentable, but that is a political decision and must be made by the participants themselves.)

There are, however, two dangers to the movement in the media's bias toward novelty and excitement. The first is the danger of rhetorical and tactical escalation in search of publicity. If this activity doesn't attract enough attention, then perhaps this one will, or this one.... The inevitable progress is from orderly demonstrations and more or less rational speeches to window-breaking, obscenity, and melodramatic calls for revolution. Steadily over time, the ante is raised, wilder things are said, greater risks accepted. Citizens come to act with one eye on what they are doing, the other fixed on its reflection in the media. They must continually astonish others in order to see themselves.

Amateur activism sometimes is astonishing, and it is always useful for a citizen to make his break with the routines of political life as dramatically as he can. But good politics most often consists in doing the same thing over and over again. Like many other worthwhile human activities, it requires a considerable capacity for boredom. This the media do not encourage, and so their influence must be opposed. The best means of opposition is the development of the movement's internal audience. Hence the need for newsletters, pamphlets, films, aimed at the membership itself and setting standards of political relevance and utility different from those established outside.

The second danger is the overexposure of movement leaders and spokesmen. One of the ways the media produce excitement is by focusing on personality. If no leader has clearly emerged, or if leadership is shared within the movement, the most colorful figure will be sought out and designated Prince. He will be filmed and interviewed endlessly, his opinions asked on a dozen different subjects, each of his performances edited so as to single out his most extravagant words and gestures, his most "interesting" self. It may be that he doesn't have opinions on a dozen different subjects, that his extravagant words represent no one else's views: it doesn't matter. Nor will he find it easy to resist the temptations of sudden fame. The movement, after all, needs publicity; if he can be its agent, has he any right to refuse the opportunity?

There are three victims here: the media audience which is entertained but not informed; the movement membership which is misrepresented; and the media Prince himself, who is all too quickly used up. He may be an exciting man, but if he keeps talking he won't be exciting for long: soon enough, someone else will be discovered. And meanwhile, other activists who trusted him as one of themselves suddenly see him in a new light: Who is he to speak so loudly? The instability of leadership among citizen activists is at least partly explicable in these terms. A man hardly has time to build a firm political base before he receives national publicity and is ruthlessly exposed to the (suspicious) eyes of his associates and followers. What can he do? Above all, he must refuse to join in the games to which he is incessantly invited, the game of *épater le bourgeois*, the game of maximal leader, the game of instant opinion. He must reflect views widely held, even if he states them in his own fashion and with his own emphasis; he must drag other people into the limelight with him; he must master the techniques of evasion and refusal.

It makes little sense, however, to refuse absolutely to face a camera or talk to a journalist. This is sometimes seen as the path of integrity. We will keep control of our own faces, activists say, and present only our unmediated selves to the world. The political purposes of the movement make that an impossible decision. One can't refuse to be described, discussed, reported. The activist has chosen to seek public effects, to influence other people, to change (some part of) their lives. He not only needs publicity; *they* deserve that his actions be publicized. So he has a public face, willy-nilly, and that inevitably means a face he can't entirely control. As a result, of course, he is not entirely responsible for his appearance. But he must take responsibility and do the best he can.

20. TACTICS

THERE are only a limited number of things to do, so it is important, first, to do them well and, second, to do them enough. Movement debates about tactics, however, rarely focus on these two imperatives. They are often disguised arguments about leaders, issues, strategies, organizational structures. And it does make sense, at least sometimes, to avoid the larger questions until they are forcibly raised by the pressures of day-to-day activity and the need for (what look like) tactical decisions. But activists should always be aware of exactly what is being decided. If canvassing is organized by ward and precinct, a future electoral campaign is being set up (and if not, not); if every local group is authorized to bring its own signs to the demonstration, a federal and, possibly, multi-issue movement is being established, and so on.

But tactics have also an interest and value of their own. Leaders and movements survive, after all, largely on tactical successes. Day after day, they must find things to do, from which activists will carry away a sense of meaning and effect and which other people also will notice and remember. What sorts of things?

CANVASSING

This is the most natural form of movement politics. Citizens talk to citizens, free for a time of the interferences of the political system and the mass media. It is most effective if the canvassers are neighbors or near neighbors, working in an area they know well. They should canvass, if possible, in groups of two, and since they will often be visiting homes where the man is away, at least one of the two should be a woman. They should be trained to avoid anger and recrimination and discouraged from involving themselves in long arguments. Argument is a most dangerous kind of self-indulgence. Canvassers come away often enough certain that they have won a major intellectual victory and left a convert. But the effect of such easy victories is usually just the opposite. Canvassing should aim at nothing more than making people aware of the movement and its issue, finding those who are already in agreement, and opening up the others to future persuasion. No one is likely to be turned around in an hour or a day, and to try to turn people around so quickly only suggests the arrogance of the committed.

Canvassers need a reason for coming to people's doors beyond the issue itself, and they sometimes want a reason for coming back. They can carry a petition or distribute a leaflet or publicize a meeting. When they find sympathizers, they should try to get them together for block or neighborhood discussions—at which a movement spokesman can be present. Most often, probably, they will be urging people to vote one way or another on a referendum statement, a candidate, or a party. Then the canvass must also serve as a poll, so that movement leaders will know where they are strong and where not. It is especially important that accurate records be kept of each encounter with a potential voter.

The value of electoral canvassing is much disputed. Clearly, it is or can be effective in getting out a large vote, but if the canvassers are working in unfriendly territory, their work may be no great gain—it may even be a real loss—for the cause. So electoral canvassing must often be limited to the movement's own constituency: it is simply a means of alerting sympathetic people to the importance of a particular campaign. It serves no other purpose; it does not extend the constituency, introduce new people to the cause, build the movement. It may not even have the effect of convincing sympathetic people of the "right" political position, since canvassers are likely to be limited in what they can say by the not-quite-satisfactory position of their candidate. Nevertheless, these are limitations worth living with, given a reasonable chance of winning the election. For victory builds the movement and extends its range faster than the most energetic and zealous canvass.

DEMONSTRATING

This is the easiest activity. It requires nothing more than that supporters of the cause get together. They must get together, however, in large enough numbers to demonstrate strength and not weakness. Demonstrations have two purposes, both of which are best served and possibly only served by numbers. They rally the activists, firing them for future work. They impress the general population, but especially its political leaders, with the power, passion, social range, respectability, or whatever of the movement.

There is always disagreement, of course, over just what ought to be demonstrated to or impressed upon the general population. A really massive demonstration is likely to require the support of a variety of political groups—sects and parties and independent locals as well as the single-issue movement itself. Perhaps the demonstration is organized by a coalition committee whose different members have quite different purposes in mind. Some way must be found, however, to establish a common discipline and a single official line, a list of speakers at the rally and spokesmen for the cause. And here the single-issue movement, assuming some minimal resourcefulness among its leaders, is by far the most likely group to win out. For it is very difficult, whatever signs or leaflets or speakers say, to demonstrate for more than one thing at a time. All sorts of arguments may be put forward at a demonstration for nuclear disarmament, say, or against this or that foreign war; the most complex ideological positions may be presented, the most provocative slogans shouted. If the occasion is right and the event itself minimally organized, all that will be remembered is that so many people turned out for nuclear disarmament or against the war.

But I don't want to suggest that signs, leaflets, and speakers are unimportant. The more complete the discipline the movement can impose, the more effective the demonstration—*for the movement* (and, presumably, for the cause). Only if the movement is or appears to be in control will professional politicians want to work with its leaders, seek their endorsement, support their political position. No one wants or needs to work with a coalition committee that doesn't even try to control its followers in any systematic way. Politicians will appeal over the heads of such a group, directly to the mass of sympathizers and activists. And these people will respond on their own, rather than as an organized constituency.

Efforts are usually made to locate demonstrations at some central point: the capital or largest city. This is obviously worth doing, but not always. A word should be said for the local demonstration. It is one of the strengths of citizen politics that it often creates significant local bases here and there throughout the country, where its part-time activists live and work full time. This is an achievement that is sometimes worth revealing, making public in some striking way. Rootedness is an impressive political fact. But the people who troop across the country for a rally in Washington or New York often look like marginal people. National demonstrations attract *demonstrators*; local demonstrations attract citizens. It is much harder, of course, to get activists to rally or march in front of their friends and neighbors, but efforts should certainly be made to persuade them to do so. The election eve parade and bonfire is a bit of old-fashioned politicking that the movement might well revive.

Planning a demonstration always involves negotiation with the police. So long as the police are willing to permit an activity more or less of the sort the movement leadership wants or hopes for, it is obviously wisest to reach agreement with them on all necessary details. Refusal by the police (or by their political superiors) may be made an occasion for disobedience, in the name of civil liberty or of the cause itself. This is an important political decision, however, and it should hang on political factors. Perhaps the most crucial of these is the kind of discipline movement leaders believe they can impose on their followers. If they have no confidence in their own authority, they probably should not challenge that of the police. A general melee most often tends to enhance the civil power, the forces of "law and order," and may lead to the repression of the movement. It will almost certainly lead to the hasty retreat of many citizen activists who had not bargained for that sort of thing at all. I suppose there are or will be occasions when such risks are worth taking, but no one should doubt the magnitude of the risks.

Demonstrations don't always require large numbers of people. They can produce effects in two other ways: when the people involved, though only a few, are already well known; and when they do surprising or dangerous or illegal things. To get a few prominent men and women to march across the city, picket a government building, or break the law in some demonstrative fashion sometimes lies within the power of the movement and is sometimes useful. For the rest, these are acts of witness, personal choices, and not tactical decisions.

STRIKING AND BOYCOTTING

These are efforts to exercise power as well as to demonstrate it, and the exercise must be effective or it is meaningless. Virtually every activist dreams at least once in his political life of winning through a general strike—the whole society (or the working class), one great rally for the cause! But except within the labor movement, even much more limited strikes are not likely options. Movement constituencies are rarely large enough, or socially located in the right way, to pull off a strike, and movement discipline is rarely tough enough to maintain it. Citizen activists will often resent claims on them that go beyond the time they have contributed. They try (not always) to keep their work lives and their family lives apart from their politics, and this is an attempt that has to be respected, even if movement leaders hope one day to involve them further. Boycotts are easier precisely because they make such minimal demands on participants.

Tax refusal and draft resistance are both forms of strikes; at least, they are so intended. I don't believe that either has ever had the desired coercive effects, for no political movement has ever been able to mobilize a large enough constituency to carry them off as strikes. But the refusal or resistance of a few people who personally accept the risks involved may be an impressive demonstration of feeling and commitment, inspiring other activists to lesser sorts of opposition. Here a great deal depends, obviously, on the public demeanor (and the public relations) of the resisters and refusers.

ELECTIONEERING

At some point the movement will almost certainly come to this, and should, with whatever misgivings. The referendum is its most obvious electoral recourse, for here it can carry its single issue directly to the mass of voters and run a "pure" campaign, unlikely to disturb its most committed members. New voters can be registered who may be useful later on. And since many citizens who won't do anything else for the cause will vote for it and even do routine election work, an organization can be built on the ward and precinct level. The independent, single-issue candidate is another easy choice. He is unlikely to win, but his campaign can serve to spread the word, and a good vote can have significant demonstration effects. (As I have already indicated, these are not entirely compatible goals.) A single-issue campaign may also put considerable pressure on one of the major parties to make the cause its own and so win the support of whatever constituency is being mobilized.

As soon as a major party does this, the movement is involved, whether it chooses to be or not, in a conventional election. It need not, however, become the mere captive of the party that adopts its cause. Now every tactical maneuver becomes important if the movement is to retain its own identity and its organizational integrity. It is especially vital that some way be found to keep control of the canvassing operation out of the hands of party regulars. The election itself may be victory enough for them, but it is at best only the next-to-last step for the movement.

All these tactics, and others too, can be employed as parts of different strategies. They can be combined in a great variety of ways, carried on simultaneously or sequentially. It is only important to remember that no one of them is in any simple sense the right thing to do; no one of them promises final victory. For this reason, tactical choices should always have two characteristics: they should be repeatable (in the way that a *Kamikaze* pilot's attack is not); and they should not have to be repeated, that is, they should not lock the movement into a particular kind of politics. Activists must always be prepared to do the same thing again and again, and be no less prepared to do something else next.

21. ENEMIES

THE PLURAL form is important. Activist citizens rarely
if ever confront a single opponent, a unified hierarchy of
professional politicians and bureaucrats, or an all-powerful
Establishment—any more than any of these confront a con-
spiracy of citizens. It is easier to take aim if one resolutely
disbelieves in plurality, but much harder to score a hit. In
fact, the movement, whatever its character, faces a variety of
enemies, who usually have considerable difficulty coordinating their resistance. They are inhibited by old rivalries, or
they disagree, much as activists do, about strategy and tactics,
or they see a chance for a little easy blackmail. It might be
that all of them would band together if the movement posed
a truly major threat. But even the history of revolutionary
struggle does not reveal that kind of unity, and, in any case,
the movement does not often pose an equally major threat
to all established groups. Indeed, it sometimes offers opportunities, above all, to leading politicians, who have often
been known to desert their traditional allies (aristocrats,
bishops, landowners, industrialists, managers) in exchange
for mass support.

Instead of presupposing enmity, on the basis of this or
that ideological vision, activists must always be on the look-
out for secret allies. Because the conventional system is itself
competitive, every intervention is bound to have different

effects on groups differently situated within it, on parties and individuals, for example, in and out of office. A massive demonstration may discredit the mayor or governor and win private applause from an opposition that would never organize demonstrations. A referendum campaign may increase the size of the election-day poll and help whatever party draws support from passive majorities. A growing movement is itself a candidate for alliances and coalitions undreamt of by its militants. These are not stable ties, to be sure, but they should never be spurned before the possibilities they open are carefully studied.

No one should be called an enemy until he has earned the title. Movement leaders, of course, must calculate their chances of winning support here or there in the society as realistically as they can. But their public stance should be open as long as openness is at all safe. They need to win support from people whose first response is worried, unsure, or hostile, and they can only do that if they avoid labeling those people on the basis of their first response. Some enemies are implacable, but that is no reason to set out to make implacable enemies.

Even if it does not seek out enemies, however, a movement may find itself fundamentally at odds with conventional moral or political standards, or with established social interests. Then it is forced to make the best of its embattled state, and since its every action is an affront or a threat to large numbers of men and women, the available options are limited. It is a great temptation, at such moments, to blame the people who are affronted and threatened. Who else is responsible for the isolation and failure of the movement? But just as seventeenth-century pamphleteers always attacked not the king but the king's advisers, so today one must attack not the people but the people's leaders. For the rest, the tasks of an isolated band of activists are obviously educational: it must put its case, doing whatever is necessary to attract some notice, but never insulting those who turn away unconvinced. It must look and sound more winning than it is.

22. THE USES OF MILITANCY

FIRST they worked within the system, and failed; then they moved outside: this is a typical activist's description of extralegal militancy. Short of revolution, however, it is not so easy to move outside. Even extra-legal actions must aim at producing effects within the system; there is no other place where effects can be had. So militant tactics must always be calculated in systematic terms. The necessary questions are obvious ones: What kind of support will they build? What kind of pressure will they put on conventional politicians? I am not going to consider here the moral implications of such questions. It is enough to point out that the commitment of activists to act as effectively as they can for the cause *is* a moral commitment. They have no right to harm their own cause, and so they must resist the pressures of personal frustration and anger that so often lead them to do so. Their calculations must be dispassionate and impersonal. These qualities are more likely the functions of organizational discipline than moral exhortation, but that only suggests the moral value of organizational discipline.

There are times when extra-legal action serves the cause. The clearest cases are those in which citizen activists already have widespread but latent support, and when all that is required for victory is the acting out of systemic values. But mass inertia, particular interests, the obstacle course of routine politics all stand in the way. Then it may well be helpful if some significant number of citizens breaks the law in order to demonstrate the importance (to them) of their cause. They say to their fellow citizens: if you don't do this or that, which you know ought to be done, you will have to put us in prison. Such demonstrations work, or sometimes work, precisely because they call attention to some common knowledge of what is right and good. Thus the history of the extension of suffrage to workers, women, and blacks: extra-legal action was effective in large part because no one watching it had good reasons (I mean, reasons they were confident about) to deny the justice of the cause. And so they were unwilling or morally unable to support a sustained program of repression and punishment directed against the activists.

When activists do confront sustained repression (as has happened often in the history of the labor movement), another kind of law-breaking may be necessary. Sometimes it is not possible to act at all, or to act with any hope of success, without setting oneself against laws (or executive orders, court injunctions, police commands) that aim explicitly at preventing collective action. Then activists break the law for the sake of reaching and mobilizing their own constituency and without any immediate reference to wider effects. Even here, however, it is wisest to act within limits, for the possibility of influencing other people should never be entirely forgotten.

People are not favorably influenced by being assaulted. Doubtless they can be forced to act in some new or different way, and if politics comes to that (to war and revolution), then one wants one's assaults to be massive. But given the hope of systemic effects, of repealing this law or changing that policy, even, simply, of ongoing political work, persuasion must be considerably more delicate. The need for caution and limit is especially urgent in the absence of common values. Then the almost certain effect of extra-legal action, and above all of violence, is to increase the distance between the band of activists and everyone else. Not only is the movement proposing new policies which many people don't understand and which they fear, but its members are pressing their proposals, acting every day, willfully and publicly, in incomprehensible and frightening ways. They may think they have moved outside the system, but in fact they have only set themselves up to be driven out. They will be driven, most likely, into sectarian isolation, where many of them will in time discover they don't want to be.

I ought to mention one further use of militance by citizen activists: they sometimes point to the violence or the threatened violence *of others* as a warning to society as a whole. There, they say to their fellow citizens, but for your acquiescence or support, go we. This is really a cry for help rather than a threat on their own part (and if a threat, not always a serious one). Like the boy's cry of "Wolf!" it can't be said too often. But there are occasions when citizen politics is only one of many possible responses to a crisis and when the others, or some of them, are dangerous to the political system (or, more often, simply to life and limb). Then the warning is plausible and may even be heeded; certainly it is worth making—soberly and quietly, if possible, as by Martin Luther King in the early 1960's. I need hardly say that it is not possible to work out in advance a division of labor between violent militants and citizen activists, so that the second group draws advantages from the outrages of the first. Nor should the activists ever pretend that if they win concessions, they can call off the militants.

23. SECTARIANISM

SECTARIANISM is the dead end of party politics within the movement. At the same time, it is a way of surviving at the dead end—even surviving for a long time—and this gives it a certain attraction.

Initially, some of the activists work out or seek out an ideology to help explain to themselves what they are doing, and why. They hold their new beliefs tentatively; they bear them lightly within the movement, cooperating with other men and women who do not share them. But then the movement suffers defeats or fails to win victories, and its participants begin to question their easy camaraderie: doesn't it conceal a refusal to face up to difficult choices, to plan for the long haul? Here is an ideology, some of them say, that describes the long haul and accounts also for our short-term setbacks, placing the movement squarely within a progressive history. Surely everyone must adopt this ideology and guide their activities in accordance with its picture of the world.

Everyone, of course, does not agree, but those who do cling more and more closely together. They begin to meet separately, distinguishing one another from the rest of the movement by their intimately shared knowledge of ideological detail. They spend much of their time testing one another, and at moments of internal crisis denouncing, purging, splitting from one another. Their willful isolation brings with it further political defeats. For each of these there is an ideological explanation. Gradually, the explanatory system becomes total, self-contained, proof against all the vicissitudes of experience. It ceases to be a way of knowing the world and becomes instead a protection against it, a hard shell within which the intense but limited life of a political sect is carried on. While the movement may well win and fade away, the sect loses and survives.

This is a model history. Obviously, it is possible to arrive at the same dead end by different routes. And along any of these there will be stopping points short of perfect sectarian isolation. Sometimes the leaders of citizen movements, clubs, or parties will even seek out some such stopping point because it offers the hope of permanence and stability, if only on the margins of the conventional political world. I mean, it establishes a political base by sacrificing something of the momentum of the movement, its thrust toward short-term resolutions of single issues. This may be a self-serving choice, but it's not necessarily that. There are important political purposes that can be served by the existence of a marginal party or a political club, like the Liberals or the Reform Democrats in New York. They can develop and try out proposals that one or another of the major parties might one day adopt; they can shift the parties (slightly) this way or that; they can reach into and mobilize sectors of society that the major parties cannot reach, and so on. In any case, survival is always a great temptation.

But what is the political purpose of surviving as a sect? It's not an accident that the word "sect" comes to us from religious history. The survival of religious sects makes sense, for they claim to fix their members in a proper relation to God. And that relation is an end in itself, a value that needn't be referred to the experience of other people. It might be better if the others shared in the relation, but better only for them. The sect member has already achieved his most important desire. This is obviously not so in a political sect. Its internal life may be marvelously vivid and intense, but it is not self-redeeming unless it redeems the others.

What often happens, however, is that the internal life of the sect becomes a substitute for all external effects. I don't mean that sectarian militants don't seek external effects. Their ideology teaches them, most likely, that they will have further opportunities to change the world, if only they cling together now and hold fast to the truths they share. Indeed, there are further opportunities, and the remnants of the last movement participate in the next. Sometimes they are able to do so in helpful ways, adopting the strategy known on the Left as the "united front," and cooperating as honestly as they can with people who don't share their faith. More often, I am afraid, they participate in the movement only in order to recruit new members for their own internal life. They have lost the commitment to single issues, the tactical flexibility, the taste for small victories—all the essential characteristics of citizen politics. They anticipate defeat and are carriers of defeat, and that is why their influence within the movement almost always has to be resisted.

24. WINNING AND LOSING

IT IS BEST to win. It is also best to appear to be winning, and since the movement is involved in an ongoing series of activities, it is usually possible to plan for a series of successes. These will mostly be small triumphs, and triumphs, perhaps, only by the movement's own measure: a successful rally, a march larger than the last march, more names on a petition than anyone expected (expectations should be low), this or that conventional politician turning around, agreeing to speak, looking for support. Such victories make the growth of the movement apparent, and movements grow, in fact, by appearing to grow. Hence the importance of the demonstration and the sequence of demonstrations, which must be aimed, above all, at communicating a sense of expansion, of numerical increase and greater social range.

There is always pressure among the activists, however, to escalate rather than expand; that is, to heighten the militancy of successive demonstrations, revealing to the country the increasing zealousness of (a part of) the movement. But escalation of this sort almost always decreases the numerical strength and narrows the social range of political action, often in disastrously sudden ways. It may even be better, though psychologically much more difficult, to move in the other direction: to lower the level of militancy over time in order to maximize growth. In any case, one appears to be winning, and one actually wins, only by reaching and involving more and more people.

It is possible to survive minor defeats, but it isn't always desirable to survive a whole series of minor defeats. If sectarian isolation is the only recourse, it is probably best to dissolve altogether and, assuming the continued significance of the cause, let some new group of people come together, differently organized, differently led, to carry on the struggle. The history of a political cause often takes this form: a number of organizations and movements, rising and falling, peaking at different points, some of them collapsing and vanishing. Only after a long time does one or another achieve enough strength to win. A history of this sort is possible because citizen activists have other things to do (other causes to work for). The movement isn't the whole of their lives, nor should it be. Activists should remember this too: they have worked hard; they can (sometimes) withdraw from the field with honor. Their part-time activity is not indispensable to the cause; the cause is not indispensable to their own lives. When a new start is necessary, it isn't or shouldn't be difficult to clear the way.

Major defeats are often caused by reaching too soon for major victories. But judgments about timing are among the most difficult of political choices. The succession of minor triumphs can't be sustained indefinitely, even by the most skillful tactician. In any case, the impatience of the activists, the demand for more decisive action, greater risks, total victory, will grow over time. Here one can only weigh internal pressure for one or another culmination against the external possibilities of achieving it. Leaders who stake everything on sudden victory are likely to be replaced, if they don't destroy the movement altogether, by leaders who lower the stakes. Those who keep the stakes too low too long are likely to be replaced by gamblers and adventurers.

Victory brings problems too. Ideally, the movement should simply dissolve, with some of its members retiring to private life, others moving on to the next cause. But victories are rarely total, and it is not always certain that they can be sustained. Then some effort must be made to hold the constituency together, to institutionalize the movement as a lobby or pressure group, to establish a foothold in the world of routine politics. This is going to look like selling out to a great many movement members. Indeed, any acceptance of victory may look like that, for activists always turn out to have hoped for more than victory brings. But it is hard to figure out a way of winning that does not involve surrendering the excitements and aspirations of fighting. And, assuming again the importance of the issue that first brought the movement together, it is better to win. There is always another fight.

25. A CALL TO POLITICAL ACTION

I WROTE in an earlier chapter that political life is different in different geographic and social locations, in different parts of the country, in different parts of the city. It also changes, obviously, from one historical moment to another. Politics is sometimes interesting, urgent, dangerous; more often, in any decent society, it is none of those things. The judgments we make of these different moments are bound to be ambiguous, and not only because some people flourish amidst urgency and danger, while others feel the full impact of the old Chinese curse: May you live in interesting times! A quiet and routine politics often conceals injustice and oppression, while "interesting times" are moments not only of risk but also of opportunity—for mobilization, revolt, social change. And citizen politics is one of the most important ways in which opportunity can be seized.

We are cursed and blessed with "interesting times." The struggle for racial equality and the struggle against the Vietnam War have mobilized large numbers of previously passive citizens, but they have also sharply divided the country, strained its political institutions, generated sporadic and increasingly serious violence. Doubtless the causes for all this lie deeper than the immediate issues suggest, though it is difficult to overestimate the extent to which the Vietnam War especially is a national disaster (and a disaster perpetrated, it should be remembered, by professionals and experts). But that is not the whole story of our troubles. The political moments of peace and equality have coincided with a more profound crisis.

In the United States today, a society whose government and economy have been progressively removed from the effective control of its citizens, or whose citizens feel themselves to be powerless and disorganized, suddenly faces a series of revolts. These are spurred by real injustices, but are not necessarily dependent on injustice for their energy and force. Very often the revolts don't have an obvious terminating point or a clear political character. Reflecting as much the general crisis as the concrete necessities of any particular cause, citizen politics has taken on the most inchoate forms, failing to achieve either national leadership or collective discipline, generating a kind of random militancy. The causes for which activists are recruited are not always the reasons, or the most important reasons, for their activities.

Nothing has a more disorienting effect upon political action than the sense of powerlessness—except, perhaps, powerlessness itself. It produces what might best be called political promiscuity, a feeling that anything goes, a desperate search for immediate if superficial effects because real effects are by definition beyond reach. And since the most desirable immediate effects are those of extremity and outrage, it produces at the same time a steady escalation toward revolutionary struggle (or, at least, revolutionary rhetoric)—as if powerlessness, which can't be overcome by increments and stages, might be transformed in one unexpected stroke. This whole style of citizen activism appeals most of all, I think, to new activists, whose escape from one or another passive role is most recent and whose sense of political possibility is barely developed. It does not serve the cause, whatever the cause is: instead, it invites the defeat and repression for which it is also a subtle kind of psychic preparation. What can the powerless hope for except defeat?

Citizen politics is not easy in the United States today; it would be foolish to pretend that it is, or to hold before the eyes of new activists the formal model of a democratic system. In almost every area of social life they are certain to encounter entrenched and efficient bureaucracies which evade, resist, wear down, or simply absorb the force of their protest. The decline of political parties and of legislative authority has clearly reduced the accessibility of the political system and made the work of newly activated citizens much harder than it once was. Nevertheless, there is abundant evidence to suggest that access is still possible and that bureaucracies can be pushed this way or that (even when they can't be seized and transformed).

A citizens' movement, carefully organized, intelligently led, can win important victories, on both the local and national levels, short of Total Victory. Both the civil rights and Black Power movements of the 1960's, and the peace movement too, had significant effects on American politics. They reached new constituencies, forced professional politicians to pay attention, built up local power bases, won changes in executive policies and bureaucratic procedures. These (small) victories ought to have been more heartening than they were, and might have been followed up in more successful ways, had there existed a larger number of activists scornful of apocalyptic talk and ready for the risks and sacrifices of an ongoing politics.

What would that look like? Why is that so hard? It requires self-control and organizational discipline, for one thing, and then the acting out of the kind of politics I have tried to describe, where every step is measured and pleasure is rarely immediate or ecstatic. It requires activists to live with and make compromises with men and women whose opinions they abhor, for no other reason than that these men and women are (temporarily perhaps) more powerful, or more numerous, or simply because they are *there*. An ongoing politics is not one whose participants can possibly hope to deliver "all power to the people" tomorrow or next month. For they represent only some of the people and must hope to win what they can win: a little more power for this or that newly organized group. And that is only possible if they work at it long and hard enough. . . .

Right now it is important to work at it long and hard. The causes for the sake of which so many of us enlisted are serious enough, but the dangers of defeat once the battle has been joined, as it has been joined in the United States today, are more serious still. It has been joined, in part, by young militants without a community base or a coherent strategy; by sectarian ideologues even more out of touch but with an all-too-coherent strategy; by isolated terrorists insanely committed to the efficacy of The Act, responsible to no one. Without the long-term activism of adult citizens, the central political movements of our time belong to them. And there is nothing more certain than that the revolution of their heated fantasies will end in a brutal and squalid repression, a bitter defeat not only for them.

The militants, sectarians, and terrorists regard themselves as the vanguard of the people; perhaps so, but they are a lost vanguard, and it is not even remotely likely that the people, whoever they are, will follow. The real question is whether citizen activists can find another way. Surely there are many thousands of Americans who will join them if they can, forging a political movement that is committed but also sane and steady in the pursuit of its goals and that makes itself an instrument as well as a symbol of democratic possibility. Nor is there any reason to think that these Americans are less fervent than those who have marched away with the lost vanguard. They are, perhaps, more modest—as befits participants in a citizens' movement. And many of them probably look forward to a time when political action is not so urgent as it is today. They are not the sort of people who will ever win glory. *But no one else can carry us forward to a society less oppressive, less unjust, more routinely democratic than the one we have now.*

OTHER NEW YORK REVIEW CLASSICS

For a complete list of titles, visit www.nyrb.com or write to:
Catalog Requests, NYRB, 435 Hudson Street, New York, NY 10014

* *Also available as an electronic book.*